T0368345

Shelter from the Storm

VOLUME ONE

RESTING IN THE PROMISES OF GOD

A Daily Devotional

ANDREW & CHRISTY MALONEY

WESTBOW
PRESS°
A DIVISION OF THOMAS NELSON
& ZONDERVAN

WestBow Press books may be ordered through booksellers or by contacting:

WestBow Press
A Division of Thomas Nelson & Zondervan
1663 Liberty Drive
Bloomington, IN 47403
www.westbowpress.com
1 (866) 928-1240

ISBN: 978-1-9736-7934-9 (sc)
ISBN: 978-1-9736-7933-2 (e)

Library of Congress Control Number: 2019918001

Print information available on the last page.

WestBow Press rev. date: 11/15/2019

Dedication

To our daughter who we lost: while our hearts grieve and our tears fall, we take comfort in knowing our great Lord will reunite us the day we meet you both face-to-face. Until that time, we leave you in your grandmother's loving arms.

⋙ Introduction ⋘

No one is immune to the storms of life: the adversities created by our relationships with family, friends, co-workers; attacks to our health, both mentally and physically; the pain of loss; the stress of work and homelife; financial distress; persecution. We live in a world system that is corrupted by sin and death, full of strife, fear and a disturbing lack of peace.

All of the difficulties that humanity faces are not unique to any one person, even those who serve the Lord. We are all pressed by life in this world—some worse than others, for sure, but we all face life-storms from time-to-time. Even the most anointed Christian, who has spent decades cultivating their relationship with Jesus Christ will sometimes feel alone, dealing with pain and despair—their very hope in God threatened by overwhelming storms that seem bent on their destruction. If you've ever felt like this, you're most certainly not alone.

It was during one of these times of great darkness that Christy and I began to feel abandoned and hopeless, seemingly left in mental anguish and, in her instance, severe physical pain. Three years later, we're still not entirely through the storm—it's been a long ordeal, and it's not been the first one we've faced, if you've read our book, *Eight Weeks with No Water.*

But just like Psalm 56:8 says, "You number my wanderings; put my tears into Your bottle; are they not in Your book?" we knew that God was not uninvolved in our plight. He sees all our tears, is moved with compassion for our pains (Matthew 14:14), and He will never leave us, nor forsake us. (Deuteronomy 31:6) Our Lord is a "Man of sorrows and acquainted with grief." (Isaiah

53:3) In the Hebrew, that is literally "pains" and "sickness." He understands what we are going through, and "surely He has borne our griefs and carried our sorrows." (Isaiah 53:4)

We may know what the Bible says about our assured victory in Jesus Christ, but sometimes that deliverance seems awfully late in coming. It was during this storm that Christy said to me, "I wish I had a devotional book that provided comforting scriptures each day, some kind of shelter when you're being beaten down and feel absolutely alone." That's where the idea of this book came from.

So Christy and I selected some of our favorite verses that brought us comfort and consolation, encouragement and reassurance, inspiration and peace—that is, shelter from the storm. We broke down each verse to really understand *what* it means, what it's saying as simply as possible, and *how* it can be applied to our lives. This book is as much for us as it is for you, but we pray it is a source of comfort to you and that it points you to the only true Shelter from the storms of life—the Lord Jesus Christ. He is your Source for everything you will ever need, no matter what circumstances you face. We pray this book helps to prove it to you.

Out of our pain and sorrow, we want to bring hope and encouragement to you during the midst of storms. Our prayer is that you will know the hope of your calling (Ephesians 1:18) and will recognize that in the midst of weakness, His strength is made perfect on your behalf. (2 Corinthians 12:9) We pray that you feel His love as you read this devotional, to know that His arms are wrapped around you to hold you up. (Jeremiah 31:3) We pray that the peace which passes understanding is manifested to you (Philippians 4:7) and that you may prosper and be in health even as your soul prospers. (3 John 2)

Hang in there! You are not alone. There is a God in heaven whose sole motivation is to share His love and power in your life. Your circumstances can change, but your LORD cannot. You *can* find shelter from the storm!

Andrew & Christy Maloney
October 1, 2019

❧ Day 1 ❧

"My soul, wait silently for God alone, for my expectation is from Him."

Psalm 62:5

O ne of the most frustrating words in the English language is "wait." The human condition hates waiting, and it's even more difficult to "wait silently." Often, we want to rant and rave about the negative situations in our lives because it makes us *feel* better momentarily. But it doesn't change the situations in the slightest and is nothing more than a form of worrying, which is the opposite of trusting in the LORD.

We must discipline ourselves not to cater to our fleshly nature by complaining. Philippians 2:14 admonishes us to "Do all things without grumbling..." The Bible shows that griping displeases the LORD (see Numbers 11:1); but thankfully, under our New Covenant in Jesus, the love of God has been poured out upon us by the Holy Spirit. (See Romans 5:5.) As we return that love to God in praise and worship, we release His power into our negative circumstances.

While it's certainly not easy to "wait silently," trusting in the Lord, offering Him worship and praise in the midst of difficulties is the best way to see your circumstances change.

1

❧ Day 2 ❦

"My soul, wait silently for God alone, for my expectation is from Him."

Psalm 62:5

*I*t's normal to want our problems to be solved quickly—it's not wrong to have this expectation; and yet, the verse just before Romans 5:5 tells us that perseverance builds character, and character builds hope. Paul goes on to say that hope won't disappoint because of the love of God. That is, the love of God is the solution to the problem.

The Hebrew word for "expectation" is literally a "cord" (Strong's #H8615), a lifeline that attaches us to God. It binds us to Him and is the grounding for our hope in Him. It is the love of God that allows us to "wait silently" until our circumstances change, and they *will* change.

Our expectation should be rooted in the love God has poured upon us by His Spirit. This unwavering, unfailing love is expressed to you by the Lord Jesus Christ: "But God demonstrates His own love toward us, in that while we were still sinners, Christ died for us." (Romans 5:8) This love is the end result of your faith and hope in Him, and if we are not convinced of His love for us, we are most certainly in for a very long wait!

✑ *Day 3* ✐

"If I say, 'My foot slips,' Your mercy, O LORD, will hold me up."

Psalm 94:18

*T*he word "mercy" here in the Hebrew is translated as "goodness, kindness, faithfulness" (Strong's #H2617) and comes from a root word that implies "to bow from the neck in courtesy to an equal." That is, to incline one's head in benevolence. Picture the King of all creation sitting on His throne, nodding specifically in your direction, treating you as an equal to His Son. That's what mercy entails!

Heinrich Gesenius, a well-respected German lexicographer, comments that, "the primary signification [of the word 'mercy'] appears to me to be that of eager and ardent desire." (See *Gesenius's Hebrew and Chaldee Lexicon.*)

The key to note here is God's "eager and ardent desire" in wanting to show us mercy. Many people in this world are under the erroneous notion that God is, at best, indifferent to their plights, or at worst, actively participating in their misery. Nothing could be further from the truth. God wants to hold us up with His mercy. He's not far from any of us, and if we grope for Him amid our difficulties, we will find Him! (See Acts 17:27.)

🕊️ *Day 4* 🕊️

"If I say, 'My foot slips,' Your mercy, O LORD, will hold me up."

Psalm 94:18

*D*avid declares in Psalm 86:5, "For You, LORD, are good, and ready to forgive, and abundant in mercy to all those who call upon You." The NIV translation says, "abounding in love to all who call to you..." God's mercy is rooted in His love for us, an "eager and ardent desire" to be generously giving of His goodness. Even in the stormy circumstances, He inclines His head toward us in compassion.

Mercy is an unchanging attribute of His existence—because God exists, there *is* mercy. Just as one cannot separate God from His holiness, neither can one separate Him from His love or mercy or healing power. We must be firmly persuaded that God *is* merciful toward us, and therefore we are upheld by that truth.

The phrase "hold me up" (Strong's #H5582) carries the definition "to support, sustain, prop up, establish, strengthen," and connotes "to refresh one's heart." It is the divine mercy of God that "holds us up" amid difficult circumstances. He is actively seeking to refresh your heart because He fervently, keenly cares for you. You must be convinced of this truth!

Day 5

"I am weary with my groaning; all night I make my bed swim; I drench my couch with my tears. My eye wastes away because of grief; it grows old because of all my enemies. Depart from me, all you workers of iniquity; for the LORD has heard the voice of my weeping. The LORD has heard my supplication; the LORD will receive my prayer."

Psalm 6:6-9

While the Lord never promises that the circumstances of life will always be easy, He does promise that it's worthwhile to serve Him, not only for the salvation of your soul, but provision in this life given in response to your faith in Jesus. So even when we cry ourselves to sleep at night, we have assurance according to His Word that He hears and receives our prayers. This shows us that our negative circumstances can change—God will intervene on our behalves, and we will come out of "dark nights."

Based on our relationship in Christ Jesus, God the Father accepts our prayers with the same fervency that He accepts His own Son's. Jesus always had His prayers answered, and we must be convinced in our spirits that the Father answers ours. The key, then, is to stand in perseverance and faith until deliverance comes—and it *will* come!

❧ *Day 6* ❧

"I am weary with my groaning; all night I make my bed swim; I drench my couch with my tears. My eye wastes away because of grief; it grows old because of all my enemies. Depart from me, all you workers of iniquity; for the LORD has heard the voice of my weeping. The LORD has heard my supplication; the LORD will receive my prayer."

Psalm 6:6-9

Tears are not weakness. God is moved with compassion by our tears, even if our faith isn't perfected. Notice the father of the demoniac child cried out *with tears*, "Lord, I believe; help my unbelief!" (Mark 9:24) Jesus did not excuse the man's lack of faith, but when He saw the father's genuine cry for help, the Lord did not leave the man hanging.

David says, "You number my wanderings; put my tears into Your bottle; are they not in Your book?" (Psalm 56:8) The Hebrew word for "wanderings" (Strong's #H5112) comes from a root signifying "grief, mourning and sorrow"—to "shake one's head" (either in agitation or with sympathy.)

Isaiah declares that Jesus is a "Man of Sorrows, acquainted with grief." (Isaiah 53:3) Rest assured that God Himself is not removed from your plight; He hears your prayers and sees your tears!

❧ Day 7 ❧

"O God, You are my God; early will I seek You; my soul thirsts for You; my flesh longs for You in a dry and thirsty land where there is no water. So I have looked for You in the sanctuary, to see Your power and Your glory. Because Your lovingkindness is better than life, my lips shall praise You."

Psalm 63:1-3

Nearly every devotional you've ever read admonishes Christians to seek the Lord "early." The word literally means "to break forth like the dawn." (Strong's #H7836) There just seems to be something to the notion of setting aside the first part of the day to minister to the Lord that sets in motion the rest of the day. Of course, we can set aside *any* time of the day to seek Him; there's nothing formulaic about rising early to spend time in prayer and to study His Word—but it takes an element of discipline to get up, say, thirty minutes earlier so you can worship the Lord. I believe God rewards one's diligence.

Regardless of *when* we spend time with God, the primary purpose for doing so should not be out of a sense of religious obligation—but truly, the demands of daily life often leave us dry and thirsty; we are worn out by the time we go to bed! We need that refreshing.

✥ Day 8 ✥

"O God, You are my God; early will I seek You; my soul thirsts for You; my flesh longs for You in a dry and thirsty land where there is no water. So I have looked for You in the sanctuary, to see Your power and Your glory. Because Your lovingkindness is better than life, my lips shall praise You."

Psalm 63:1-3

The word "longs" (Strong's #H3642) implies "to faint with longing" once we've encountered the presence of the Lord. Once we've tasted and seen the Lord is good (see Psalm 34:8), it creates such intense desire to have "more" of Him, that we pine without Him. According to Fairuzabadi, a fourteenth century lexicographer, the Arabic cognate refers to paleness of skin due to pining, wasting away till the skin becomes pallid. Without the dawning light of the Son, even our skin color fades!

After the new birth, we know our bodies become the temple (sanctuary) of the Holy Spirit (see 1 Corinthians 6:19) and the power and the glory of the Lord is housed within us. (See 2 Corinthians 4:7.) Truly, God's lovingkindness (that means, goodness, mercy, favor) is better than life and all its demands! It is so good that God Himself has taken up residence within your spirit—praise Him with your lips, praise Him early!

Day 9

"They are abundantly satisfied with the fullness of Your house, and You give them drink from the river of Your pleasures. For with You is the fountain of life; in Your light we see light. Oh, continue Your lovingkindness to those who know You, and Your righteousness to the upright in heart."

Psalm 36:8-10

Sometimes I like the way the King James phrases scripture, even if it's a little harder for modern readers. In Verse 8, David uses the word *deshen* (Strong's #H1880) which we translate "fullness," but is more closely rendered "fatness," which is what the KJV uses. The word refers to the fat that is melted and mixed with the ashes of a sacrifice upon the altar. In olden times, they would fertilize their fields with this mixture of fat and ashes, yielding an abundance come harvesttime.

David waxes poetic, using the metaphor of drinking from the river of [God's] pleasures, suggesting that being a member of God's household gives us plenty of "food and drink" (fat and water, as it were.) Not only natural sustenance, but more importantly, ample spiritual nourishment. Not just the essential nitty-gritties of physical and spiritual life, but even the delightful, fancy things that aren't necessary for survival.

❧ *Day 10* ❧

"They are abundantly satisfied with the fullness of Your house, and You give them drink from the river of Your pleasures. For with You is the fountain of life; in Your light we see light. Oh, continue Your lovingkindness to those who know You, and Your righteousness to the upright in heart."

Psalm 36:8-10

The word "pleasures" here means "luxuries, dainties, delights, fineries," and is the word for the Garden of "Eden." (Strong's #H5730) God's not just interested in meeting your most basic of needs—but He is the Fountain of Life, the overabundance of *everything* good, even the Light we so desperately need to grow and thrive as people. It is all found in Him: fatness, water, sunlight, even the little "dainties" we like to nibble on.

Recognize during your daily life (which, of course, is not always lounging in the sun, by a river, eating bon-bons!) that God is spilling over with lovingkindness, exploding with righteousness. That word means "justice, vindication, prosperity." (Strong's #H6666, #H6663)

Rest assured you can find shelter in the storms of life abiding in the household of God!

✠ *Day 11* ✠

"As for me, I will see Your face in righteousness; I shall be satisfied when I awake in Your likeness."

Psalm 17:15

While most of us, unlike David, do not have physical enemies encompassing us—rebel kings, bloodthirsty assassins, treasonous subjects, and the like—it often feels like we are surrounded by circumstances and, indeed, some *people* who wish to do us harm. We all have enemies of some sort, physical and/or spiritual, who are like lions with their heads bowed down, ready to spring upon us. (Verses 11-12)

However, what's so powerful about this prayer is that David is firmly persuaded he is justified in presenting this petition of deliverance to the LORD. He declares his faith in God, which has made him righteous. He declares in Verse 3 that God has proven his heart, and that he does not make this prayer with "feigned lips." (Verse 1) When we face the "enemies" of life, we too need to have this understanding: we are righteous before the LORD because of our proclamation of faith in Jesus Christ.

❧ *Day 12* ❦

"As for me, I will see Your face in righteousness; I shall be satisfied when I awake in Your likeness."

Psalm 17:15

We know David was not without his faults; he did some pretty awful things in his lifetime. In himself he could not cull the favor of God, but it was because of the "marvelous lovingkindness" of the LORD that he had an expectation of God's deliverance for those who "put their trust" in Him. (Verse 7)

The phrase "I will see Your face" carries the connotation of a king's prerogative to "see" someone into his throne room, to grant access to "behold" his royal presence; to be favored with an audience before the king. The "face" of the Lord is the part of Him that "turns toward" us with kingly favor. (Strong's #H6440; #H6437)

This access is based on "righteousness" (Strong's #H6664), which here means "vindication of a just cause in a controversy." David was confident God would rule in his favor against his enemies. He knew he would be "satiated in excess" when he "startled from sleep" in God's "manifestation of favor." (Strong's #H7646, #H6974, #H8544)

*"Glory in His holy name; let the hearts of those rejoice who seek the Lord!
Seek the Lord and His strength; seek His face evermore! Remember His
marvelous works which He has done, His wonders, and the judgments
of His mouth…"*

1 Chronicles 16:10-12

The word "glory" (Strong's #H1984) is from a root meaning "to be clear," like a clarion call or a bright color shining forth. It speaks of *boasting* of God's holy name, exulting almost to the point of frenzy. The word is translated "mad" on eight occasions. We're to be loud, boisterous—we should *REJOICE* because we seek the Lord and His strength, His face forevermore.

The troubles and tribulations of this life are sent by the enemy to wear us out. (See Daniel 7:25.) Sadly, so many Christians are coasting through life because they are simply exhausted by the pressures and vexations of day-to-day living in this corrupt world system. Yes, some of their problems are self-made, but many of them seem beyond their control.

In turn, have we lost a little bit of that zeal and reckless abandon we once had in our love of the Lord? We *must* get it back!

❧ *Day 14* ❧

*"Glory in His holy name; let the hearts of those rejoice who seek the LORD!
Seek the LORD and His strength; seek His face evermore! Remember His
marvelous works which He has done, His wonders, and the judgments
of His mouth..."*

1 Chronicles 16:10-12

So how are we supposed to keep that wild, unrestrained "glorying" in the Lord's strength? Part of the answer is remembering "His marvelous works." We're instructed to recall the things we have seen the Lord do in the past—things above the norm; special, "separate" acts (over and above the "regular things.") The word "wonders" refers to the "beautiful things" (Strong's #H4159, #H3302) our Lord has done, even the execution of His righteous decrees (that's "judgments") on our behalves.

I am very confident that each of us, as children of God, can think of at least *one* instance where we have seen Him do something special and beautiful for us.

You're born again, aren't you? That's the most special and beautiful thing God has ever done for humanity. We do well to remember His works and *glory* in the power given to us through His name!

14

☙ *Day 15* ❧

"Return to the stronghold, you prisoners of hope. Even today I declare that I will restore double to you."

Zechariah 9:16

The word "return" (Strong's #H7725) most succinctly means "go back to," but it also carries the connotation of being restored, refreshed, and is elsewhere translated "requite, recompense, render, recover." Being paid back for something lost. In fact, it is the same word used to represent the phrase "I will restore" in this verse.

The Hebrew word translated "stronghold" (Strong's #H1225) is unique throughout the Old Testament to just this one verse. It suggests our English word "bastion" and is formed from a root meaning "inaccessible by height, fortified." (Strong's #H1219)

While this prophecy is literal for the Israelites of Zechariah's time, we can apply a spiritual principle to "returning to the stronghold" in our lives today—that is, abiding and not moving from a place of secured position under the unassailable protection of our Lord Jesus Christ. (See Psalm 91:1.)

☙ *Day 16* ❧

"Return to the stronghold, you prisoners of hope. Even today I declare that I will restore double to you."

Zechariah 9:16

*P*risoners (Strong's #H615) is taken from the root meaning "to be hitched or yoked (to something)"—in this case, hitched to "hope" (Strong's #H8615), which, as we've said elsewhere, is "a cord or rope," an attachment to our expectations of being recompensed for what was taken from us. We should all be prisoners of hope!

The Lord certifies a restoration to these prisoners of hope double-fold what was lost. A hundred percent, and a hundred percent again, given back to them for the troubles they have faced. Even amid the storms of life, we should consider ourselves prisoners of this hope for a double blessing, a total turnaround of circumstances, that are always subject to change, from the One who never turns, never changes. (See James 1:17; Malachi 3:6.)

If Almighty God declares He will cause us to recover double for our troubles, we can rest assured He is fully capable to make good on His promises!

❦ Day 17 ❧

"My voice You shall hear in the morning, O Lᴏʀᴅ; in the morning I will direct it to You, and I will look up."

Psalm 5:3

Many Christians, when faced with the adversities of life, cry out to the Lord in a sense of desperation. That's not necessarily wrong. Our circumstances sometimes make us feel as if we are just keeping our heads above water. But it is important to recognize we need to seek the Lord with an *expectation* to hear from Him. Oftentimes, we can reach out to Him but not really have an expectancy to hear *back* from Him. We are not calling out to Him in faith.

In Hebrews 10:38, the Lord admonishes us: "Now the just shall live by faith; but if anyone draws back, My soul has no pleasure in him." "The just shall live by faith" was a primary concept of Martin Luther's reformation based on his reading Romans 1:17, copied from Habakkuk 2:3-4: "For the vision is yet for an appointed time; but at the end it will speak, and it will not lie. Though it tarries, wait for it; because it will surely come, it will not tarry. Behold the proud, his soul is not upright in him; but the just shall live by his faith."

⊰ Day 18 ⊱

"My voice You shall hear in the morning, O Lord; in the morning I will direct it to You, and I will look up."

Psalm 5:3

While most of us have a "vision" (of deliverance, of healing, of prosperity, of restoration, etc.), even though it tarries until the "appointed time," we are instructed to "wait for it"—that means to have a sense of hope and expectation for its arrival. It is in this context that the "just shall live by faith."

When David directed his voice to the Lord in the morning, notice that he "looked up." That Hebrew word (Strong's #H6822) means most properly "to lean forward," to "peer into the distance" and "wait for" something. It's translated twenty times in the Old Testament as "watchman."

When David cried out to the Lord, he waited to hear something back—he had an expectation, a "vision" of his deliverance, and a faith in God that it would come to pass. When you go through the storms of life, remember, even though it may tarry, wait for the vision to come to pass. Expect it! The just live by faith!

Day 19

"Cause me to hear Your lovingkindness in the morning, for in You do I trust; cause me to know the way in which I should walk, for I lift up my soul to You."

Psalm 143:8

*C*ause me to hear" carries the connotation of not only attentively listening but also obeying. Our relationship with the Lord is directly influenced by our level of trust in His leading and in turn promptly obeying that leading. To the level that we seek to hear God's voice and obey His direction is the level to which we can navigate the storms of life. That doesn't mean we *avoid* all storms, but we are carried through them safely and quickly.

God has the most direct route to getting us through any situation we might face. James 1:5-6 promises that He will give wisdom liberally to anyone who asks in faith. But if we do not put that wisdom into action, it does us no good. That's why James later says, "Therefore, to him who knows to do good and does not do it, to him it is sin." (James 4:17)

You *can* hear God's voice. The question is what will you do when you hear it?

❧ Day 20 ❧

"Cause me to hear Your lovingkindness in the morning, for in You do I trust; cause me to know the way in which I should walk, for I lift up my soul to You."

Psalm 143:8

"Cause me to know the way" speaks not only of knowing our duty—what God expects from us, our calling and obligations before Him (and we all have them!)—but also that He would give us divine knowledge on how to fulfill that duty, safely and efficiently. This speaks of a children of Issachar anointing (see 1 Chronicles 12:32), to understand the times we live in and a strategy to know how to navigate them effectively.

God knows the best way. It behooves us to know His way early in the journey (whatever situation we are facing.) That's what "in the morning" means poetically: to get God's thoughts on the matter sooner rather than later. Sometimes, one of the reasons our circumstances can seemingly last so long is we didn't seek His wisdom from the outset and immediately put it into motion by our obedience. We did not "understand the times."

"Lift up my soul" speaks of laying our personal desires before the Lord, surrendering our will to His, because He knows what's best for us.

ᵈᵏ Day 21 ᵏᵉ

"So teach us to number our days, that we may gain a heart of wisdom. Return, O LORD! How long? And have compassion on Your servants. Oh, satisfy us early with Your mercy, that we may rejoice and be glad all our days!"

Psalm 90:12-14

*E*ven when we've "messed up" and are in the midst of a crisis of our own making, either by outright disobedience or neglecting to implement His wisdom, we've got to keep a proper perspective in knowing that God takes no pleasure in our suffering. He does not grieve or afflict the children of men from His heart. (See Lamentations 3:33.) His compassion toward us is unwavering and without end. His mercies are new every morning. (See Lamentations 3:22-23.) If we return to Him, He "returns" to us.

In reality, He didn't move in the first place, *we* did. But once we are back in line with Him, God will continue teaching us to "number our days." The context of this phrase is found in the earlier verses where Moses is outlining God's eternality contrasted to our own mortality. Understanding that He's got it "all figured out," and we most certainly do not, is one of the first steps to gaining a "heart of wisdom."

❧ Day 22 ❦

"So teach us to number our days, that we may gain a heart of wisdom. Return, O LORD! How long? And have compassion on Your servants. Oh, satisfy us early with Your mercy, that we may rejoice and be glad all our days!"

Psalm 90:12-14

"How long?" I cannot be the only person besides Moses who's asked this question before. Our storms of life often seem to take so much longer to get out of than they did to get into! Sometimes we know why we're in the midst of a storm, sometimes we do not. And while I believe the Lord wants us to know *why* in just about every case, and we should seek Him to learn the reasons, His response toward us is the same in either case: He has compassion on His servants.

While the Bible calls us friends (John 15:15-17) and children of God (1 John 3:1), we are also "unprofitable servants" simply doing our duty. (Luke 17:10) Paul called himself a "bondslave" of Jesus Christ. (Romans 1:1) We serve the *King*, and while we may not get all the answers we want at the time we want it, our King will satisfy (excessively surfeit) us with His mercy, so we can be joyful all the days of our lives. What a great God we serve!

❧ Day 23 ❦

"The LORD is my strength and song, and He has become my salvation. The voice of rejoicing and salvation is in the tents of the righteous; the right hand of the LORD does valiantly. The right hand of the LORD is exalted; the right hand of the LORD does valiantly."

Psalm 118:14-16

Strength in the Hebrew comes from a root "to prevail" (Strong's #H5810) and speaks of hardening, to make strong, to become stout. This verse declares that strength comes from the LORD. The ability to overcome adversity is resident within God's power, not ours, and we are strengthened by Him alone. When Romans 8:37 declares we are "more than conquerors" it is *through* Him who loved us. It is God who "causes us to triumph" *through* Christ. (2 Corinthians 2:14) Jesus told us, "I am the vine, you are the branches. He who abides in Me, and I in him, bears much fruit; for without Me you can do nothing." (John 15:5)

What is one of the keys to abiding in Christ? The psalmist clues us in: "The LORD is my song." That word implies praise, singing psalms, and instrumental worship. (Strong's #H2176) Seems almost too simple, but it is a fundamental truth: through continuous praise and worship, abiding in Him, we are made strong, stoutly hardened against adversity.

Day 24

"The LORD is my strength and song, and He has become my salvation. The voice of rejoicing and salvation is in the tents of the righteous; the right hand of the LORD does valiantly. The right hand of the LORD is exalted; the right hand of the LORD does valiantly."

Psalm 118:14-16

"Right hand of the LORD" is a poetical description of God's inherent strength. Since most people are righthanded, the right side of the body was traditionally considered "stronger and more dexterous." (Strong's #H3225) Therefore, we would say the power of the LORD is "exalted," or high and lofty, lifted up and raised against our adversity, ready to strike. (Strong's #H7426) The word "valiantly" signifies power and might, specifically of a warlike nature. (Strong's #2428) It means to "show oneself strong" and is often translated as the word for "army."

The right hand of God gives the righteous "salvation." This word is *Yeshua* (Strong's #H3444), which you'll recognize as the Hebrew for Jesus. His name speaks of deliverance, health, welfare, and liberty. In fact, the root word connotes having "ample space" to move about, freedom. It is in His power to set us free from our afflictions, and this is what causes the "voice of rejoicing!"

Day 25

"'Now therefore, I pray, if I have found grace in Your sight, show me now Your way, that I may know You and that I may find grace in Your sight. And consider that this nation is Your people.' And He said, 'My Presence will go with you, and I will give you rest.'"

Exodus 33:13-14

Paul gives the primary goal of every Christian in Philippians 3:10: "...that I may know Him and the power of His resurrection, and the fellowship of His sufferings, being conformed to His death..." To have an ever-increasing experiential knowledge of Jesus Christ: His power, His sufferings, His death and resurrection. Notice that this relationship with Him doesn't exclude you and me from the same adversities He faced (Matthew 5:11; 1 Peter 3:14), but the point here is Jesus' power through you, overcoming any difficult circumstance. It is to the level that you "know" Him, His ways, His will, His purposes, that the level of His grace is manifested to you. When going through the storms of life, it's important to recognize the cause of the difficulty: Is it demonic? Is it living in a fallen world system? Is it from poor decisions we've made? Is it the persecutions we face by following Christ? In each case, God's grace will be established in your circumstances as you grow in your knowledge of Him.

❧ *Day 26* ❧

"'Now therefore, I pray, if I have found grace in Your sight, show me now Your way, that I may know You and that I may find grace in Your sight. And consider that this nation is Your people.' And He said, 'My Presence will go with you, and I will give you rest.'"

Exodus 33:13-14

While Jesus does tell us we will have tribulation in the world, we should be of good cheer because He has overcome the world. (John 16:33) Now, I am compelled to point out that sickness, disease and untimely death are not "tribulations," they are a result of the curse of sin in the world. (See Micah 6:13; Romans 5:12.) Thankfully, Jesus has overcome the world, broken the curse, and paid a tremendous price to bring you healing. (See Isaiah 53:5.)

"But where sin abounded, grace abounded much more, so that as sin reigned in death, even so grace might reign through righteousness to eternal life through Jesus Christ our Lord." (Romans 5:20-21)

What is grace? God's presence going with us, giving us rest. That word means "to settle down and remain in repose." (Strong's #H5117) It is in God's presence that we find rest from our tribulations. This is why it's so important to "know" Him and His ways.

❧ *Day 27* ☙

"And He said to me, 'My grace is sufficient for you, for My strength is made perfect in weakness.' Therefore most gladly I will rather boast in my infirmities, that the power of Christ may rest upon me."

2 Corinthians 12:9

No one likes undergoing trials, and while I am convinced that many storms of life could be avoided by listening for and immediately obeying God's wisdom, the fact remains that we'll all have circumstances in our lives we'd rather not have. We live in a world system that is corrupted by the effects of sin, and we are not fighting against flesh and blood, but against a spiritual enemy (Ephesians 6:12), who would like nothing more than to thwart the purposes God has for us by wearing us down with these negative situations. (See Daniel 7:25.)

However, God has initiated a seeming paradox within this world system to ultimately prove His total authority in every condition. It is in the midst of our frailty that His strength is shown perfect, and we find ourselves able to face the challenges with a grace that is not our own. In the natural, most of us would be utterly overpowered by the ordeals we face, and yet because of God's power flowing through our lives, we are able to bear up under them and, in time, overcome them. Don't forget this truth!

❧ Day 28 ❧

"And He said to me, 'My grace is sufficient for you, for My strength is made perfect in weakness.' Therefore most gladly I will rather boast in my infirmities, that the power of Christ may rest upon me."

2 Corinthians 12:9

*G*od's answer to Paul was just as valid, even though it wasn't what he wanted to hear. However, it was Paul's *response* that solidified the reward: the power of Christ resting on him. "I'm weak, but God's power flows through my weakness." There's much debate on what those "infirmities" were. The Greek word signifies both soulish and bodily weakness, a lack of strength. (Strong's #G769) I maintain that perpetually laboring under physical sickness is *not* God's will for His children in some effort to "perfect" His strength in their lives. However, the paradox of God's power showing through our infirmities (weaknesses) is a biblical truth.

While you are pressing into God for physical healing (and you should!), or waiting patiently for Him to correct those negative situations in your life, do not lose sight that, in acknowledging your weakness—that in yourself, you cannot "fix" whatever's wrong—the door is opened for God's miraculous power to flow through.

Day 29

"But God has chosen the foolish things of the world to put to shame the wise, and God has chosen the weak things of the world to put to shame the things which are mighty; and the base things of the world and the things which are despised God has chosen, and the things which are not, to bring to nothing the things that are, that no flesh should glory in His presence."

1 Corinthians 1:27-29

*H*ere's another paradox that God created in His kingdom: some of things we consider the strongest, He calls the weakest; what we think is "wise," He calls foolish. He's done this so that no one can boast in themselves. Isn't it true that the people who have the most—the strongest, noblest, richest, smartest—often have the most difficulty in accepting the Lord Jesus Christ? His grace is available to them as much as to the poor, humble weakling, but their advantages are often stumbling blocks to accepting that grace.

God *does* wants you to have a prosperous journey in life. (See 3 John 2.) It brings Him no glory for one of His children not to have enough money to feed themselves! But we would be wise to remember in His kingdom, the economy is backward to human thinking.

❧ *Day 30* ❦

"But God has chosen the foolish things of the world to put to shame the wise, and God has chosen the weak things of the world to put to shame the things which are mighty; and the base things of the world and the things which are despised God has chosen, and the things which are not, to bring to nothing the things that are, that no flesh should glory in His presence."

1 Corinthians 1:27-29

*B*alance is needed to distinguish between the seeming backward economy of God's kingdom and the equal truth that we can do "all things" through Christ. (Philippians 4:13) Many people, while piously trying to remain "foolish, weak or base," labor under a lifetime of burdens God never intended for them to continue in. Yes, we all begin weak and ignorant, but God doesn't want us to *stay* that way. He uses the pressures of those foolish, weak things to draw us toward Him, so that His strength can blast through, turning those circumstances into wise and mighty things. To make the things "which are not" into "things that are" and vice versa.

We should not remain "are nots" our whole lives! Jesus' prayer in Matthew 11:25 was to show those "hidden things" were revealed to babes, but not that we should remain babes forever! (See Hebrews 5:12-14.)

❧ *Day 31* ❧

*"But I am poor and needy; yet the L*ORD *thinks upon me. You are my help and my deliverer; do not delay, O my God."*

Psalm 40:17

*P*oor in the Hebrew (Strong's #H6041) can refer to lacking money, but the word more closely relates to "weak and wretched," especially in the sense of pious regard: humility before the LORD. The root means "to stoop;" that is, bent over with affliction, to be occupied in the mind, downcast, depressed. The word "needy" (Strong's #H34) is the feeling of want, to suffer "oppression and abuse," and was a description of the lowest caste of society: beggars. David is basically saying here, "I feel like a pitiful, kicked around beggar." He recognized he had no remedy for this condition without God's deliverance. Haven't we all felt like this sometimes? Pressed down by our circumstances, bowed down under the cares of our lives?

But also realize the LORD *thinks* of you. How amazing, that in all of creation, you are in God's thoughts! Yes, you! He will not forget you. (See Deuteronomy 31:6; Hebrews 13:5.) He will not abandon you. Though mankind may fail you, your God will not. This is a truth of inestimable comfort when you feel "poor and needy."

✥ Day 32 ✥

"But I am poor and needy; yet the LORD thinks upon me. You are my help and my deliverer; do not delay, O my God."

Psalm 40:17

No negative circumstance or sorrow is too great to bear so long as we keep the bedrock truth that God thinks upon us and has sent His Comforter (the Holy Spirit) to help us in our weaknesses. (See Romans 8:26.) It is when we neglect this truth that we begin to despair. This is how Paul can make such a statement in 2 Corinthians 4:8 and still talk about the "excellence of God's power," a treasure pouring out of an earthen vessel.

The word "help" is Ezra (Strong's #H5833), meaning succor, which is "comfort and aid." "Deliverer" here carries the connotation of making one "smooth and sleek"—like a calf that is delivered from its mother's womb (see Job 21:10)—to assist one in "slipping away" and escaping out of danger. (Strong's #H6403) God's help makes us "slide" through the difficulties we face. David ends his prayer with a sincere plea for God not to delay in sending His deliverance. This should be our prayer, also, but kept in the context David had: a *confidence* that God will indeed deliver us as He delivered David.

*"Come and see the works of God; He is awesome in His doing toward
the sons of men."*

Psalm 66:5

The first clause of this verse is a command that is two-fold:
1) to seriously consider and meditate on God's works, and
2) to have a proper attitude toward them: giving God praise
for those mighty works. (See Psalm 150:2; Luke 1:49.) It's not
just a casual, cursory glance: "Right, God's works are good,
yeah, okay." But to stop and *really* take note. "Oh, what God has
done!" (Numbers 23:23) This is a wise thing to do for our *own*
benefit. And once we have done so, to credit God in glory and
worship for them.

When we truly consider the works of God as seen through
the perfection of Jesus Christ as the sum of the Father's complete
thought toward mankind, we cannot help but be awestricken in
admiration for His goodness. Salvation, deliverance, healing,
provision, mercy, grace, love, justice, and stability—Jesus gives
it all.

We have a whole lot to be thankful for!

❧ *Day 34* ❧

"Come and see the works of God; He is awesome in His doing toward the sons of men."

Psalm 66:5

*A*wesome in the KJV is translated "terrible" in the archaic context of causing astonishment and shock (as opposed to the modern sense of "bad"), and in the original Hebrew, it is the word for "fear," but it carries the connotation of reverence and respect. (Strong's #H3372) Conversely, "children of men" is a phrase employed to show the immeasurable difference between God Himself and the people He created. The phrase is often used in contrast to "children of God" to make a distinction between those who follow Him and those who follow their own ways. We are made in the image of God. (See Genesis 1:26-27.) Image means "shadow" or "resemblance." (Strong's #H6754) Like a carbon copy.

While we may *look* like God regarding our physical likenesses, we must not forget that He is entirely Other in His substance. What makes Him God is an inherent power and worth (His glory) that we cannot replicate, but merely receive and reflect. While this is *terrible* in the old-fashioned sense of the word, it is also comforting because we know He is above all our circumstances, and therefore, able to change them. How awesome!

Day 35

"Finally, my brethren, be strong in the LORD and in the power of His might."

Ephesian 6:10

This verse opens Paul's discourse on the "whole armor of God": truth, righteousness, peace, faith, salvation, and the Word of God coupled with praying in the Spirit. All these elements must be incorporated into our daily walks in order to fulfill the commandment: "be strong in the LORD." We could render "be strong" as "strengthen yourselves." That means we should fulfill our duty as Christian soldiers in the Lord's army by courageously and consistently taking care of our *armor*—living daily in truth, righteousness, and peace. That is how salvation (deliverance) comes: through studying God's Word and praying in the Spirit, mixing it all with faith.

In order to press our spiritual rights under the Lord's new covenant, we must be diligent in not neglecting our soldierly duties to ensure our armor is in top condition. Have you considered your armor today? Be sure to take time to put it in order!

❧ Day 36 ❧

"Finally, my brethren, be strong in the LORD and in the power of His might."

Ephesian 6:10

While it's true *we* have certain duties and obligations to be diligent and dauntless in our application of the armor of God, Paul is careful to point out it is "in the LORD" that we can be strong. Our strength comes from Him. One of the bedrock standards of the Bible is: in and of ourselves, we are incapable of walking in righteousness, peace and salvation. Even our faith is instigated and completed by God. (Hebrews 12:2) We're standing in the power of *His* might, not ours. But how is His strength and power communicated to us? By applying the truths of the "armor of God" to our circumstances. This application is two-fold: 1) through persistent, accurate study of God's Word, and 2) through powerful prayer in the Spirit (that is, the baptism of the Holy Spirit with the evidence of speaking in tongues.) It takes both principles operating in tandem in order to see total victory in every area of our lives. Many sincere, well-meaning Christians often neglect one or the other and end up with only a partial victory. I believe it was with this intent that Jesus said: "You are mistaken [deceived], not knowing the Scriptures nor the power of God." (Matthew 22:29 [brackets author's own])

❧ *Day 37* ❧

"Only fear the LORD, and serve Him in truth with all your heart; for consider what great things He has done for you."

1 Samuel 12:24

Samuel is here trying to teach the children of Israel the "good and right way" (Verse 23) to please the LORD after they'd "done all this wickedness" (Verse 20) in asking for a human king to be placed over them. See, the children of Israel weren't content with the LORD being their unseen, spiritual Monarch, speaking through the mouths of His prophets. They wanted a physical representation as their head of state. How often are we in today's world alike! If we can't see it, taste it, touch it, we treat it as immaterial, and therefore, somehow not as worthwhile. So many people would rather have the golden calf, than the true power of an invisible God. (See Exodus 32.)

The LORD is a Spirit. Subsequently, He must be worshipped "in spirit and truth." (John 4:24) Equally true, the power and strength that He provides must be appropriated spiritually before we can wield it naturally (physically) against our negative situations.

❧ *Day 38* ❧

"Only fear the LORD, and serve Him in truth with all your heart; for consider what great things He has done for you."

1 Samuel 12:24

Just because we don't see a change in the natural the moment we pray doesn't mean that God hasn't already set things in motion in the spiritual realm. Don't lose your focus on the spiritual at the expense of the natural! But how can we do this? It's hard to say, "I know spiritually I'm healed," when in the natural, you're still sick. Samuel again gives some solid advice: 1) fear only the LORD. (Isaiah 8:13) Don't fear the natural, reverence only God, give Him the first place in your thinking always. (See Luke 4:4-7, 22-34.) 2) Serve Him in truth with all your heart. (See Deuteronomy 6:5.) "In truth" means without pretense, or false piety in obligation, but from a willing heart because what else do you do with God except serve Him? 3) Consider what great things He has done for you. This is important: take stock and review all the times throughout history and in your life that He has benefited you and those around you. This is vital in "converting" the spiritual truth into power and strength in the natural. These principles help make the *real* become the *reality*.

❧ *Day 39* ☙

"Be angry, and do not sin. Meditate within your heart on your bed, and be still. Selah. I will both lie down in peace, and sleep; for You alone, O Lord, make me dwell in safety."

Psalm 4:4,8

*W*hen faced with unpleasant circumstances, it's natural, human response to become angry. God understands emotion, as He is the Originator of all emotion. If you can become angry or happy or sad, so can He. He possesses the same range of feelings as you. Therefore, your emotions are not "evil." They just shouldn't *rule* over you.

That phrase "be angry" is more literally "tremble or quake with agitation (in anger or fear.)" (Strong's #H7264) David, here, is saying, one can be agitated and still not be "in sin." Paul quotes this phrase and further says, "Do not let the sun go down on your wrath, nor give place to the devil." (Ephesians 4:26-27) The apostle is saying don't give the enemy an *opportunity* in your life through unbridled emotion.

Rather, we're admonished, when we lay down, to "meditate within our hearts." That means, process our emotions (Strong's #H3824) and learn to "be still."

☜ *Day 40* ☞

"Be angry, and do not sin. Meditate within your heart on your bed, and be still. Selah. I will both lie down in peace, and sleep; for You alone, O LORD, make me dwell in safety."

Psalm 4:4,8

*B*e still" is the Hebrew word *damam* (Strong's #H1826), which is the same root as "still" in 1 Kings 19:11-12. Combined with *daq* (Strong's #H1851) we get the "still, small" voice of the LORD. This passage is showing, during the storms of life (the wind, the earthquake, the fire), God's voice is heard "still and small."

One must be quiet themselves to hear a quiet whisper. It's when we are "meditating within our hearts" that we begin to perceive the direction of the LORD in a still, small voice. This is why a lot of revelation from the Spirit comes in the night hours, when we are quiet and still, when our emotions are calmed, when we ourselves are *daq damam.*

It is a decision we make to "both lie down in peace and sleep," to choose not to let our emotions steal the "safety" God wants us to dwell in. The LORD alone gives that safety, but we must choose not to remove ourselves out of it through unchecked, "loud and large" emotion.

❧ Day 41 ☙

"I will love You, O LORD, my strength. The LORD is my rock and my fortress and my deliverer; my God, my strength, in whom I will trust; my shield and the horn of my salvation, my stronghold. I will call upon the LORD, who is worthy to be praised; so shall I be saved from my enemies."

Psalm 18:1-3

*S*trength in this passage is represented by two words. The first is the only use in the Old Testament meaning strength in the sense of providing "help." (Strong's #H2391) The second means "a sharp rock" or a cliff/bolder with a precipitous edge. (Strong's #H6697) It goes alongside David's use of "rock" which properly means a "lofty crag"—up high and safe. (Strong's #H5553) The word "trust" means to "flee," to run to safety and take refuge. (Strong's #H2620) "Fortress" comes from the root for "a hunter's net," meaning to be caught up, ensnared or captured into safe keeping. (Strong's #H4686)

There is a principle set forth here that the Lord's help (strength) comes when we run to Him. He catches us up and places us in a high and lofty place, where we are delivered from the attacks of life. The key to all this is our act of fleeing *toward* Him, staying in intimacy and communion with Him.

❧ Day 42 ❧

"I will love You, O Lᴏʀᴅ, my strength. The Lᴏʀᴅ is my rock and my fortress and my deliverer; my God, my strength, in whom I will trust; my shield and the horn of my salvation, my stronghold. I will call upon the Lᴏʀᴅ, who is worthy to be praised; so shall I be saved from my enemies."

Psalm 18:1-3

"Fleeing to the Lᴏʀᴅ" comes in the form of communion, intimate worship and praise, with Him. Sunday morning service is not enough time in a week to keep ourselves in the high and lofty place of safety from the pressures of our daily lives. David recognized that calling upon the Lᴏʀᴅ, who is worthy to be praised, was a vital component to his life's safety. He worshipped consistently, constantly. Paul tells us to, "Rejoice always, pray without ceasing, in everything give thanks; for this is the will of God in Christ Jesus for you." (1 Thessalonians 5:16-18)

It was in this lifestyle of worship that David had the confidence to call the Lᴏʀᴅ his shield or buckler. The etymology of the Hebrew word for "shield" means to "cover over and surround" completely. It's also the word for the scales of a crocodile's hide. (Strong's #H4043) Jesus is the "Horn of salvation." (Luke 1:69) Spend time in His presence, and you *will* be saved from your enemies!

❧ Day 43 ❧

"The LORD is my strength and my shield; my heart trusted in Him, and I am helped; therefore my heart greatly rejoices, and with my song I will praise Him."

Psalm 28:7

God is the Source of all strength, the Creator and Possessor of it. This strength encompasses not only physical vigor, a strong, healthy body; but also mental strength to deal with the pressures of life and to control our emotions, so that they do not rule over us. It is this strength "on loan" from God that is our shield, which protects the areas of our lives where we are most fragile and susceptible to attack.

And all of us have places that are more fragile than others, not just in our physical bodies; but in certain "mind-blinders," areas of our thinking which are not fully illuminated by the Word and the Spirit of truth. The Bible calls this the "infirmity or weakness of our flesh." (See Romans 6:19 and 8:26.) Again, while it can refer to physical infirmity, it also speaks to areas of our minds that are still "darkened" in the understanding of who God is and what He represents to us. (See Ephesians 1:18.) This is a lifetime process of growing in our relationship with Jesus, which all starts with our "hearts trusting in Him."

❧ *Day 44* ❧

"The LORD is my strength and my shield; my heart trusted in Him, and I am helped; therefore my heart greatly rejoices, and with my song I will praise Him."

Psalm 28:7

*T*rust can only be set in one Person to overcome those "infirmities of our flesh"—that is, the Lord Jesus Christ. We've all learned through life experience that trusting in humanity can only take us so far. People will fail us, even those with the best intentions, even our family and friends, from time to time, because they also have "infirmity" in their flesh. And we certainly should have learned by now that we cannot trust in *ourselves*. If we think we have life "all figured out," we are deceiving ourselves. Therefore, the only Source in which to deposit our full trust is God Himself, who never has an "infirmity of the flesh" moment.

How does trust in God "help" us? It enables the divine aid of God's limitless strength to flow through every situation. This help is not always instant, but it is always timely, coming in many ways: direct intervention (miracles), through someone God sets in our path, sometimes through the natural order of things "working themselves out." Don't miss the supernatural looking for the explosively spectacular!

❦ *Day 45* ❦

"The LORD will give strength to His people; the LORD will bless His people with peace."

Psalm 29:11

*P*salm 29 often sounds like the "soundtrack" of our lives, doesn't it? Waters, and thunders, and broken trees, fires and earthquakes—the storms of life, as it were. Except, notice David's point here: even though God is *in* the midst of these storms with us, He is the One ruling *over* them; they don't influence Him in the slightest. That is not to say He is the Source of the storms of life—that comes from this world system and its occupants, but He is God even over the fires and quakes and floods. He sits enthroned as "King forever." (Verse 10)

In these verses, the psalmist king is reminding his people (and us) that even though the storm rages, God is the Shelter in the midst of the storm. Even the most "mighty ones" (Verse 1) among us are commanded to give—that is, "ascribe"—to God the glory and strength that is due to His name in the beauty—that is, "majesty"—of holiness. We are told to worship Him in the midst of the storm.

❧ Day 46 ❧

"The LORD will give strength to His people; the LORD will bless His people with peace."

Psalm 29:11

For those who "worship the LORD in the beauty of holiness," there is a tremendous promise that closes out this psalm. This promise is only made to "His people," those who choose to trust the Lord alone for salvation and righteousness, wholeheartedly pursuing a relationship with Him. Jesus, in His discourse against worrying, states: "But seek first the kingdom of God and His righteousness, and all these things shall be added to you." (Matthew 6:33)

"All these things" is summed up in the definition of peace, which in the Hebrew is the word *shalowm*. (Strong's #H7965) It comes from a root meaning "to be whole or entire" and encompasses much more than just the absence of war. It means to be "happy, safe, well, prosperous, sound, tranquil, healthy, content, favored." This is the strength of the LORD on display to His people—that they are blessed with peace. And keep in mind, this is all in the context of being "at peace" amid the storms of life. This is His promise to you!

❧ *Day 47* ❧

"And let us not grow weary while doing good, for in due season we shall reap if we do not lose heart. Therefore, as we have opportunity, let us do good to all, especially to those who are of the household of faith."

Galatians 6:9-10

One of the primary fruits of righteousness is peace. (See Hebrews 12:11.) We become the righteousness of God when we put our faith in Jesus alone. (See 2 Corinthians 5:21.) And while this fruit is not reaped based on any of our own works—it is the gift of God (see Ephesians 2:8-9)—there is still the equally true premise that "faith without works is dead." (See James 2:14-26.) The Law of Sowing and Reaping is not "done away with" by our faith in Jesus Christ; rather, it is completed, expressed and expanded by it. (See Matthew 5:17-20.) Because you are at peace with God, in right-standing with Him based on your relationship with Christ, you will be compelled to "do good" and display your faith and peace to those around you.

You may be going through the storms of life, but so is everyone else. No person is exempt from the pressures of day-to-day life. However, one of the greatest means of reaping peace in your life is in the service of others, especially your brothers and sisters in Christ. We need you!

❧ Day 48 ❧

"And let us not grow weary while doing good, for in due season we shall reap if we do not lose heart. Therefore, as we have opportunity, let us do good to all, especially to those who are of the household of faith."

Galatians 6:9-10

Faith that is "dead" means it's ineffective, "inactive, inoperative, deprived of power" (Strong's #G3498), if we are not bearing fruits worthy of our repentance. (See Matthew 3:8.) We must plant good works in faith in order to reap the harvest of peace during storms. A seed lies dormant until it is placed into the ground; it does not grow without work. The good news is, just like a seed, the power inherent in faith is not lost when it is dormant. If we stir it back up, we can still reap a harvest. "Doing good" is not only giving tithes and offerings to the local church (although this is important.) We can sow time into the lives of others: family and colleagues. A heart attitude of praise and worship, gratitude and thanksgiving, is sowing in faith as well. Most of us do not have full-time ministry positions, but we all have ministry expressions to offer to those around us. Find someone to bless, even with just your kind words, and you will be "doing good." With an attitude of sowing in faith, we are assured a reward of peace amidst our own troubles.

❧ Day 49 ❧

"And God is able to make all grace abound toward you, that you, always having all sufficiency in all things, may have an abundance for every good work."

2 Corinthians 9:8

Constant progression is implicit in this verse: steps building upon one another. Firstly, the ability of God is made *available* to you (see Romans 4:12) as a manifestation of grace. He not only can but will.

Secondly, grace in the Greek is *charis* (Strong's #G5485), which in turn comes from a root used as a greeting meaning "Godspeed," or more specifically "be cheerful, glad, calm, happy and well off." So "all grace" is *everything* that would make a person all the above descriptions. Grace in all its many facets unreservedly.

Thirdly, this "all grace" *abounds* toward you. This verb means to flourish, proliferate, swarm, overflow—thronging, teeming, brimming overfull. The exact definition of the Greek word (Strong's #G4052) is "to exceed a fixed number of measure, to furnish so richly there is an abundance." The word is used to describe a flower going from bud to full bloom, to blossom. Any way you slice it, that's a *lot* of grace made available to you!

❧ *Day 50* ❧

"And God is able to make all grace abound toward you, that you, always having all sufficiency in all things, may have an abundance for every good work."

2 Corinthians 9:8

What is the purpose of this "all grace"—the ability of God—abounding to us in overabundance? We are not blessed just for the sake of being blessed, though of course, we reap the benefits of grace ourselves. But rather, we are given grace so we might be sufficient in all things. All means "all." (What revelation!) But sufficiency (Strong's #G841) means self-satisfied, contented, "a perfect condition of life in which no aid or support is needed."

Why does God give us all sufficiency? To have excess for every good work (that is, honorable, useful enterprises.) Grace above measure, so that which is overflowing can be passed on to others. More than enough, so we can meet the needs of others. It means more than just money. Sufficient to meet the needs of others, whatever they may be lacking: love, joy, peace, healing, emotional wellness, whatever the case may be. Being graced to help alleviate the storms of others in turn helps alleviate ours. This is a vital principle to a lifestyle of peace. "So shines a good deed in a weary world."

❧ *Day 51* ❧

"Because he has set his love upon Me, therefore I will deliver him; I will set him on high, because he has known My name."

Psalm 91:14

C ashaq (Strong's #H2836) is the Hebrew word represented as "set his love upon Me." A word study shows it to mean "joined together," and could be rendered "cleave or adhere to" or "delight and long for." It is the same word used to describe something being "banded together," or archaically "filleted," with silver. It means to "be attached to" in the strongest manner. We might say nowadays "attached at the hip" or "fall in love with."

It is interchangeable with a similar Hebrew word (Strong's #H2820) that means "restrain, hold back for oneself, refrain, withhold, reserve," in the context of keeping ourselves *for* God alone, and keeping ourselves *from* evil. Being separated solely unto the Lord, filleted to Him, bound to Him, and preserved from falling apart by our great love for Him.

Deliverance through and from the storms of life is directly tied into "setting our love" upon Him. The closer we are to Him, the less we are affected by the things going on around us.

⁂ *Day 52* ⁂

"Because he has set his love upon Me, therefore I will deliver him; I will set him on high, because he has known My name."

Psalm 91:14

For those who have fallen in love with God, He promises to "set them on high." This word (Strong's #H7682) means "exalted, lifted up" to a high place that is inaccessible and safe. It is the same word used in Proverbs 18:10: "The name of the LORD is a strong tower; the righteous run to it and are safe."

There is a place we can reach in our love relationship with God wherein we are "out of reach" from the snares and cares of this world. It doesn't mean that there *aren't* snares and cares out there; it simply means we're too tightly tied up with God for them to catch or affect us.

Very few of us have attained that kind of relationship with God yet, but it doesn't negate the truth that we can *all* get to that high and lofty place in our walk with Him. We come to this place by "knowing His name." That phrase means intimacy, learning to love, His name—His true character, reputation, authority, fame and glory.

❦ *Day 53* ❦

"Wait on the LORD; be of good courage, and He shall strengthen your heart; wait, I say, on the LORD!"

Psalm 27:14

There's that word again: wait. We don't like this word in English. Waiting in line, waiting for the light to change, waiting for our circumstances to get better, sitting around, waiting... It can carry a sense of dread, having to do something we'd rather not do. Hurry up and wait!

But in the Hebrew it carries a different connotation. It means to "bind or twist together" (Strong's #H6960), and it implies being strengthened like taking strands of twine and twisting them together to make a rope. We might say today "gather up your strength." Waiting, in this context, is not passive, but active: looking forward eagerly with expectancy and hope.

We are admonished *not* to "wait" like we would in the lobby of a dentist's office, but rather to anticipate zealously the intervention of the Lord into our daily circumstances. One is waiting for Christmas morning; the other is waiting for a root canal. I don't know about you, but I'd rather "wait" in the first kind of sense than the second!

❧ Day 54 ❧

"Wait on the LORD; be of good courage, and He shall strengthen your heart; wait, I say, on the LORD!"

Psalm 27:14

Isaiah 40:31 tells us, "But those who wait on the LORD shall renew their strength; they shall mount up with wings like eagles, they shall run and not be weary, they shall walk and not faint."

There is a principle in "renewing strength" during the storms of life that is found in waiting on the LORD. The act of waiting creates the "wings" and "feet" to fly or run through the storm. It seems that most of us do not wait upon Him nearly as much as we should—and I include myself in this statement.

"Waiting" upon Him indicates an attitude of submission and humility, as the servant waits upon the master—one who is there for His bidding, to learn what He desires and place ourselves in the position to accomplish those desires. It's more than just "sitting and waiting"—but making ourselves available to serve Him. We do this by dedicating ourselves to obedience in prayer and worship, then sitting in silence, waiting to be commanded by the King.

Be of good courage and dedicate a portion of your day to waiting upon Him!

❧ *Day 55* ❦

"I will cry out to God Most High, to God who performs all things for me."

Psalm 57:2

*G*od Most High" (Strong's #H410, 430, 5945) describes the most supreme Being, One who is superior to all else, and therefore in a lofty position to do "all things," that is, *anything*. Although the words "all things" are not in the original Hebrew, it is implicit by the title ascribed to Jehovah, He who is "Most High" is able to do exceedingly, abundantly above all we can ask or think. (Ephesians 3:20)

We do not serve a mute idol, some block of wood or stone, or a false god whose demands for worship are based on an "or else!" attitude with nothing given in return. The true God Most High is a loving benevolent, all-powerful Spirit.

Many people in the world, including a lot of Christians, have a veiled understanding of who God Most High is, some angry taskmaster or petulant tyrant with a list of rules to follow. Yes, He does demand you approach Him His way—there are things He expects you to do, and not to do; but God is a rewarder of those who diligently seek Him (Hebrews 11:6), and He is most certainly in a position to reward us with "all things!"

❧ Day 56 ❧

"I will cry out to God Most High, to God who performs all things for me."

Psalm 57:2

Performs is perhaps better translated as "complete, finish or perfect." (Strong's #H1584) The word implies the ability to finish what He has started, but it is more than ability—it is trustworthiness and faithfulness that God does nothing halfway. In fact, since God is timeless and eternal, knowing the end from the beginning (Isaiah 46:10), the very fact that He has started something for you already shows He has completed it for you. He never begins something without already finishing it. *Selah.*

God is as good as His Word. (Psalm 138:8) It is a finished deal, all of the long history of Earth and all its belabored inhabitants—yes, every storm you will ever face has *already* been overcome by the One who promises to "perform all things" for you. How comforting!

"God is not a man, that He should lie, nor a son of man, that He should repent. Has He said, and will He not do? Or has He spoken, and will He not make it good?" (Numbers 23:19)

❧ *Day 57* ❧

"We are hard-pressed on every side, yet not crushed; we are perplexed, but not in despair; persecuted, but not forsaken; struck down, but not destroyed..."

2 Corinthians 4:8-9

Keep in mind Paul was imprisoned when writing these letters. He understood what it meant to be "hard-pressed." That word is interesting in the Greek; it comes from a root "to rub or wear" as in a well-worn, rutted path and was used to define "pressing" grapes for wine. (Strong's #G2346; #G5147) Literally and figuratively it means "to be crowded in upon," compressed, narrowed, straitened.

Do you sometimes feel almost suffocated by the burdens of life pressing in around you, be that from circumstances or people themselves? Recognize you aren't alone; nearly every person you encounter is "pressed" in their own ways. But that isn't nearly as comforting as recognizing the truth that you are not alone *because* God has not forsaken you, any more than He did Paul in prison. (Deuteronomy 31:6; Hebrews 13:5) Your LORD is with you in thick and thin, take heart!

"For a righteous man may fall seven times and rise again..." (Proverbs 24:16)

"We are hard-pressed on every side, yet not crushed; we are perplexed, but not in despair; persecuted, but not forsaken; struck down, but not destroyed..."

2 Corinthians 4: 8-9

Perplexed means "not knowing the way to go." (Strong's #G639) Just because we sometimes don't know "what to do" about a current situation, that does not mean we need to despair. Certainly there is an element of trust a sailor puts into his or her ship as they're tossed willy-nilly through the ocean's upheavals, believing their craft will weather the storm and keep them afloat.

This analogy bears well through the storms of life, but even more so, since our "Ship" is not made by man's hands out of wood or metal—God cannot founder amidst storms that are so far insignificant considering His greatness, as to be nothing more than a fleeting moment. That's not to demean whatever storm you're facing, but we need to recall His perspective when it seems our lifeboat is about to be swamped.

If we don't know the way to go, we can trust our great Navigator knows the way and will carry us through. You can trust your Captain with your life. (1 Peter 1:3-5)

"Trust in the LORD with all your heart, and lean not on your own understanding; in all your ways acknowledge Him, and He shall direct your paths."

Proverbs 3:5-6

*B*atach is the Hebrew word for "trust," a root word meaning "to move quickly for refuge," (Strong's #H982), trusting in the security of that refuge to keep one safe. It means "careless," boldness, not in the sense of acting rashly or foolishly, but rather, not to permit the attacks from outside to shake one's confidence that they are secure in their place of refuge. We are told to put this kind of trust in the LORD with all our hearts (our minds and souls and willpower; see Strong's #H3820.)

This decision to be "careless" can sometimes seem contrary to the human drive of self-preservation. The Bible does not tell you to wholly cast away that survival instinct and go do something ignorant, but rather to submit that drive to God's direction and wisdom. That's what the verse above means by "lean not..." Your own understanding (that is, knowledge) is faulty and incomplete—but God's is not. You must surrender that drive to *control* what goes on around you, recognizing your inability to do so, while the LORD's ability is not lacking one bit!

❧ *Day 60* ❧

"Trust in the LORD with all your heart, and lean not on your own understanding; in all your ways acknowledge Him, and He shall direct your paths."

Proverbs 3:5-6

Preaching to myself, I think one of the greatest shortcomings Christians in general have is not "acknowledging Him" in all their ways. How often have we made a decision that very well could alter the course of our lives without properly submitting that decision to the Lord, getting His thoughts and ideas about it? It seems in many cases, a lot of the storms we face have been because of decisions we've made, giving very little thought to what God might have had to say on the subject. Not because of out-and-out rebelliousness, but simply because, "We know what we're doing." And most of the time, with the benefit of hindsight, it's clear we had *no idea* what we were doing.

Now, we can take this so far where we're afraid to choose what we want for lunch without submitting it to God in prayer. He created you with a brain to make decisions and expects you to use it. However, it does not negate the truth that when it comes to serious choices in life, we would all be a little wiser to take the time to acknowledge Him and allow Him to direct our paths.

"I know how to be abased, and I know how to abound. Everywhere and in all things I have learned both to be full and to be hungry, both to abound and to suffer need. I can do all things through Christ who strengthens me."

Philippians 4:12-13

A *based* in this passage is "humbled, lowly in heart, not rising far from the ground." (Strong's #G5013) Abound, on the converse, is "to exceed, to be furnished so richly there is abundance." (Strong's #G4052) These conditions appear like polar opposites, but oftentimes, these conditions are not "either or" but both. In one area of life, we seem to be riding the crest of the wave; in another, we're drowning in the trough. This is not a unique position to any person. (1 Peter 4:12-13) We're all susceptible to times of abasement, or abounding, often mixed all together.

The point here is that Paul *learned* how to be content in all circumstances. Contentment does not come naturally. This word is used only once in the NT, and it comes from a root meaning "hidden, secret purpose." (Strong's #G3466) It's where we get the English word "mystery," and is translated "instructed" in the KJV. This means God teaches us His "secret counsel" to learn serenity "everywhere and in all things."

❧ Day 62 ❧

"I know how to be abased, and I know how to abound. Everywhere and in all things I have learned both to be full and to be hungry, both to abound and to suffer need. I can do all things through Christ who strengthens me."

Philippians 4:12-13

I don't know how nonbelievers cope with the storms of life without the comfort and strength of Jesus Christ. I think life would be absolutely horrifying if all I had to rely on for my well-being is my fellow man and government institutions. I'm "proud" to admit my reliance upon the direction of the Word of God and the Holy Spirit!

It's only through Christ's strength we can learn to do "all things." Without that vibrant relationship with the Lord, when people are faced with extreme adversity, they are often left with only two responses: anger (at themselves, at others, or at God, if they happen to believe in Him) or apathy, retreating within themselves, and simply "giving up," learning to exist rather than truly living. Conversely, when people have times of abundance, without Christ, they become pompous, overbearing and self-centered. Let's *learn* by leaning upon Christ and relying on His strength in all circumstances!

❧ Day 63 ❧

"But may the God of all grace, who called us to His eternal glory by Christ Jesus, after you have suffered a while, perfect, establish, strengthen, and settle you."

1 Peter 5:10

Jesus stated a fact in John 16:33: "You will have tribulation..." But He also stated, "In Me you may have peace." This is sometimes an overlooked component of "all grace" that is given to us by God: the grace to have peace in the midst of storms "by Christ Jesus." Often, we think of grace as demonstrative: Jesus dying for our sins and thereby forgiving them by His shed blood, settling forever the enmity that the Father had toward His rebellious creation. And that is all completely true: grace is unmerited favor given to an unworthy recipient based on His goodness, not ours.

But another component of His grace conveyed to us through Jesus is the ability to "hold up" under pressure and adversity, to "suffer graciously" for a season of time and come through the ordeal un-embittered by the experience. It is as much a work of grace that He has forgiven you your sins, as to give you peace in contrary situations the world throws your way. Don't forget His grace is sufficient for you! (2 Corinthians 12:9)

❧ Day 64 ❧

"But may the God of all grace, who called us to His eternal glory by Christ Jesus, after you have suffered a while, perfect, establish, strengthen, and settle you."

1 Peter 5:10

A while in the Greek signifies "little, small, few," and speaks of a "short duration" or a "slight degree of intensity." (Strong's #G3641) God derives no pleasure in dragging out your suffering or piling misery upon misery. (Lamentations 3:33) While He may *permit* for a season certain levels of adversity so that you might learn reliance upon His strength through Jesus Christ, the reason is not to torment you because He likes it when Christians suffer. That demeans the work of Christ suffering in your stead! If His grace is sufficient for us, wasn't Christ's suffering equally sufficient?

Rather, when we yield to His grace, the storms of life 1) perfect; 2) establish; 3) strengthen; and 4) settle us. *Perfect* is "to render fit, sound, complete, to mend and make one what he/she ought to be." (Strong's #G2675) *Establish* is "to make firm, constant, stable." (Strong's #G4741) *Strengthen* means "bodily vigor." (Strong's #G4599) *Settle* means "to lay a foundation." (Strong's #G2311) The same word is used in Matthew 7:25; Ephesians 3:17; Colossians 1:23; and Hebrews 1:10.

❧ *Day 65* ☙

"And we know that all things work together for good to those who love God, to those who are the called according to His purpose."

Romans 8:28

*K*now most literally means "to see with the eyes," and by implication "to perceive by experience." (Strong's #G1492) That is, to know something tangibly because you've lived through it. It's not to be some ethereal concept: "Someday, maybe when we get to Heaven, things will be 'all good.'" It's intended to be an experience in *this* life. This statement is a biblical promise, and as such, is one hundred percent true. However, I'm sure many of us know Christians for whom "all things" don't seem to be working together for good. Why the seeming discrepancy?

The answer is found in the previous passage. (Romans 8:26-27) It is in this context of the Spirit's intercession *through* us (primarily through our praying in tongues) that He makes intercession *for* us according to the will of God. We could phrase it this way: it is the intercession that is *inspired* (or breathed on) by the Holy Spirit that is effective in making "all things" work together for good. When facing the storms of life, it cannot be overemphasized the importance of our heavenly prayer language!

⊰⊱ *Day 66* ⊰⊱

"And we know that all things work together for good to those who love God, to those who are the called according to His purpose."

Romans 8:28

The promise of "all things" working for good does not mean Christians won't ever have bad situations. *All things* means "all things" (good and bad.) Rather, it means all things can be *synergized* ("work together;" Strong's #G4903) for good by the power of the Spirit to "help in our weaknesses." (Verse 26) This applies only to the Saints who love God, those people in covenant with Him by their faith in Jesus Christ. The word *called* means "invited," as when one bids another to come to a banquet—here it means "divinely selected and appointed." (Strong's #G2822)

Purpose is interesting. (Strong's #G4286) It is the word used for "showbread"—the twelve wheat loaves "shown" before God continually in the Temple, refreshed every seven days, and consumed in a holy place by the priests, signifying communion together with God. Those working with the intercession of the Spirit are those who are "shown" before Him constantly, called according to His purpose. It is those people to whom all things work together for good.

❧ Day 67 ❧

"Have I not commanded you? Be strong and of good courage; do not be afraid, nor be dismayed, for the LORD your God is with you wherever you go."

Joshua 1:9

*I*magine being Joshua here. Your friend and mentor, the leader of the entire people, has just died; and after four decades of wandering, you're now tasked with the daunting commission of conquering an entire land filled with enemies. Does this constitute as "the pressures of life"? I daresay it does, and then some. I don't think any of us has faced these kinds of circumstances. I'm sure, naturally speaking, Joshua would've preferred to be in just about any other place at that moment, otherwise why would God have needed to encourage him?

The principle here is that all of us at one time or another will be facing a situation we'd much rather not deal with. Our initial response could either be one of fear or one of dismay—these are natural reactions to seemingly overwhelming circumstances. When this happens, we must remember that we don't face the problem on our own with only natural, human effort. Even if we don't know the solution, have faith in God, trust Him to lead you through it as the Source of all your supernatural strength, wherever you go.

❧ *Day 68* ❧

"Have I not commanded you? Be strong and of good courage; do not be afraid, nor be dismayed, for the LORD your God is with you wherever you go."

Joshua 1:9

*H*ave I not commanded you?" is a key part in this scripture. Joshua wasn't thinking this plan up on his own. The previous eight verses constitute a command to action based on a plan conceived and executed by God Himself. Notice the LORD placed limits on Israel's conquest. (Granted, the land He'd given them was *very* great.) We all have a designated area of operation where we can enforce our rights against the enemy: health, provision, family, work, etc. Often, it's when we step outside our sphere of influence that we face the most adversity. We must know God's plan in any given situation for Him to be with us "wherever we go." The promise is conditional. The command in Verse 8 gave power to the promise of Verse 9.

Being "strong and of good courage" is contingent upon following the prompting of God. This doesn't mean God can't "bail you out" when you get yourself into a mess, but you may undergo a lot more stress than He ever intended. Be wise and obedient, and *then* be strong and courageous, confident that your steps are directed by His leading, instead of solely your own.

⋙ *Day 69* ⋘

"Those who sow in tears shall reap in joy. He who continually goes forth weeping, bearing seed for sowing, shall doubtless come again with rejoicing, bringing his sheaves with him."

Psalm 126:5-6

*J*ust about everyone is familiar with the concept of sowing and reaping. The phrase, "You reap what you sow," is in the common lexicon as a proverb meaning "what you put in, you get out," usually as an admonition: we all face the consequences of our actions, good or bad.

"Do not be deceived, God is not mocked; for whatever a man sows, that he will also reap. For he who sows to his flesh will of the flesh reap corruption, but he who sows to the Spirit will of the Spirit reap everlasting life." (Galatians 6:7-8)

When going through the storms of life, we must always keep this principle in mind. Our decisions (good or bad) directly influence what we will get out of any particular situation we face (good or bad.) "Therefore, to him who knows to do good and does not do it, to him it is sin." (James 4:17) This principle is important: if you want a good harvest, sow good seed, always. It really is as simple as that.

❧ Day 70 ❧

"Those who sow in tears shall reap in joy. He who continually goes forth weeping, bearing seed for sowing, shall doubtless come again with rejoicing, bringing his sheaves with him."

Psalm 126:5-6

However, this passage in Psalms adds another layer to the proverb, *You reap what you sow.* Here we see a promise that God will take sown tears and provide a bounty of joy. This, like all biblical promises, isn't a blanket statement. The tears must be sown in faith that there *is* a harvest of rejoicing coming. We must ensure the tears we shed over our negative circumstances are not tears of frustration, fear or self-pity.

But the principle is there. Our tears do indeed move the hand of God when sown with a proper heart. Reference the father of the epileptic child in Mark 9:24. My own father once said, "It's one thing to pray over a need; it's quite another to weep over it!" Personally, I don't think we weep over our situations as often as we should. When facing life-storms, if you are moved to tears, make sure they are tears sown in faith, expecting to bring your sheaves of joy back with you. It's okay to cry—that's not weakness—just make sure you are crying the right way.

❧ *Day 71* ❧

*"Peace I leave with you, My peace I give to you; not as the world gives
do I give to you. Let not your heart be troubled, neither let it be afraid."*

John 14:27

The promise of peace in this verse is more than just platitude;
it comes from the Originator of peace, the Prince of peace.
(Isaiah 9:6) Ephesians 2:14-15 says that Jesus Christ "made
peace" by gathering Jews and gentiles together in Himself as
"one new man." Peace is more than absence of hostility, it is
"security, safety, prosperity, felicity (because peace and harmony
make and keep things safe and prosperous.)" (Strong's #G1515)
So while the greatest definition of God's peace is reconciliation
to Him through the new birth, it also carries over into the
believer's day-to-day life. You're not supposed to have peace just
when you go to Heaven—it's to be a condition of your existence
in *this* world. It is very beneficial to accept Christ's offer of peace
sooner rather than later.

Even when the storms rage around you, you can be tranquil
and calm, safe, prosperous, even *happy*, rooted in the assurance
that Christ's peace is your possession. "…And the peace of God,
which surpasses all understanding, will guard your hearts and
minds through Christ Jesus." (Philippians 4:7)

"Peace I leave with you, My peace I give to you; not as the world gives do I give to you. Let not your heart be troubled, neither let it be afraid."

John 14:27

*T*he world does not give a lasting peace. All governments, families, friendships, plans and schemes, ultimately provide fleeting peace because they are based on *people* who are looking for the same peace you are. The definition of world is given as, "the whole circle of earthly goods, endowments, riches, advantages, pleasures, etc., which although hollow and frail and fleeting, stir desire, seduce from God and are obstacles to the cause of Christ." (Strong's #G2889) This is all the world can offer you in the name of peace.

Notice "Let not..." indicates there is a decision on your part to accept and live in God's peace—it doesn't happen automatically any more than salvation of the soul does. You have a role to play in a lifestyle of peace. It is only when we actively decide to live in Christ's peace, on His terms, apart from what the world is offering us, that we can begin to "let not our hearts be troubled or afraid." You *can* choose not to be agitated or fearful when trials come your way. It takes faith and discipline, but peace is attainable on this earth for every child of God.

❧ *Day 73* ❦

"Be sober, be vigilant; because your adversary the devil walks about like a roaring lion, seeking whom he may devour."

1 Peter 5:8

*S*ober and vigilant" means "self-controlled and watchful." Thayer's defines sober as "temperate, circumspect." Vigilant means "wary, on alert." Have you ever known a Christian who it seemed they almost *insisted* they get the "entitlement" to worry about situations entirely out of their control? I think some people define themselves by their calamity—they begin to identify with the contrary circumstance.

Others are so lackadaisical in their approach to God that they respond to trials in the same way as the people of the world: just throw up your hands and switch on the TV. Apathy is just as dangerous as running around like a maniac, pitching a fit.

The *correct* way to approach the storms of life is as one who is moderate and unruffled in their emotions, but also as one heedful and attentive in their faith towards God. It takes both attributes—temperance and vigilance—to keep a proper perspective on the things that come our way. These are commands from God to be obeyed immediately and at all times.

❧ Day 74 ❧

"Be sober, be vigilant; because your adversary the devil walks about like a roaring lion, seeking whom he may devour."

1 Peter 5:8

Your adversary is a defeated foe. Christ's crucifixion and resurrection stripped the devil of power (Colossians 2:15, as just one example), save what we choose to yield to him. Your enemy must rely on tricks, deceit and subterfuge (John 8:44; 2 Corinthians 2:11) to get you to yield him power that is yours by right, based on your relationship with the risen, conquering King.

Many well-meaning Christians live a lifestyle of fear, worry and doubt—all of it based on the lie that the accuser of the brethren (Revelation 12:10) is stronger than they are.

That's not to say the devil can't roar quite loudly, but he can only pounce and bite when you walk into his open mouth. We must be "sober and vigilant" so that we do not walk into a trap out of intemperance or indolence in our thoughts, emotions, speech and actions. Don't allow the storms of life to trick you into believing your accuser is *ever* telling the truth. Jesus assures us, he's *not*!

❧ Day 75 ❧

"Resist him, steadfast in the faith, knowing that the same sufferings are experienced by your brotherhood in the world."

1 Peter 5:9

So how do we battle our adversary? Actually, the battle is not ours—it's the LORD's (2 Chronicles 20:15), and He's already crippled your enemy by His victory at the cross. Satan's head (that is, his authority) has already been crushed. (Genesis 3:15) All we're waiting on now is death's final defeat at Jesus' second appearing, which is the culmination of this age. (1 Corinthians 15:26)

That's not to say we don't have a "battle" on our hands. But it is a battle of willpower, played out in the arena of our minds, wills and emotions, not some physical confrontation of strength. We *wrestle* against spiritual forces, this is true (Ephesians 6:12), but how we fight the enemy is through steadfast *resistance.* This is why Hebrews 12 talks about "running a race with endurance"—not hacking at a foe far more powerful than we are. Our double-edged Sword (the Word of God) is just as sharp for cutting through our issues as it is the enemy. (Ephesians 6:17; Hebrews 4:12) Our role as soldiers in the army of the Lord is to *resist* a paralyzed foe with endurance. Don't exceed your standing orders!

❧ *Day 76* ❦

"Resist him, steadfast in the faith, knowing that the same sufferings are experienced by your brotherhood in the world."

1 Peter 5:9

Resist in the Greek is *anthistemi* (Strong's #G436)—yes, it looks like the allergy medication. The word means "to set oneself against," and in this verse it is in the imperative (command) sense. The same for James 4:7: "Therefore submit to God. Resist the devil and he will flee from you."

The Lord would not issue you a command and not give you the inward power to execute it; therefore, it *is* possible to resist the onslaught of the enemy. No person who belongs to God is forced to do the enemy's bidding. But it requires an act of will that is set steadfast in faith—unmovable in our expectation that God *will* cause the enemy to flee.

This struggle of the wills is not unique only to you. Every Christian, at certain times, will be required to exercise their rights over the enemy by choosing to resist his lies and tricks. Take comfort in knowing that all of us face the storms of life together. But take greater comfort in knowing your God has empowered you to resist them!

❧ Day 77 ❧

"But you, be strong and do not let your hands be weak, for your work shall be rewarded!"

2 Chronicles 15:7

The context of this command is a prophecy given to Asa, king of Judah, from Azariah. Asa was instructed to overthrow idolatry, and that would restore peace throughout his domain. While Asa was not a perfect king, especially in the latter years of his reign, he set to this directive to purge the land of idols with a will, even going so far as to depose his own grandmother for idol-worship. His obedience to this prophetic mandate ushered in thirty-five years of peace, so much so that many northern Israelites in the tribes of Ephraim and Manasseh migrated to Judah. His holiness unto the LORD became an attractive beacon to his brethren around him. While today's Christian is not likely to offer worship to Asherah on some "high place," the principle for us remains the same just as in Asa's time. Idolatry equals a lack of peace. It is possible (not strictly mandatory) that some of the storms of life come our way because we have placed something above our commitment to the Lord—this is modern idolatry. While we should not live our lives in a constant state of critical self-examination, we should consider if some "idol" has allowed the peace to depart and the storms to roll in.

❧ *Day 78* ❧

"But you, be strong and do not let your hands be weak, for your work shall be rewarded!"

2 Chronicles 15:7

Strong is this verse means "to take courage, be urgent, be resolute, hardened," that comes from a root meaning "to fasten upon, to seize." (Strong's #H2388) There is nothing apathetic in this command. I like that the word for "hands" also metaphorically speaks of support, in the sense of axles or tenons. The idea here being our foundation must be resolute and unwavering, being quick to tear down any "idols" that the Spirit brings to our understanding.

While we may not be committing out-and-out sin, we all have areas of our lives that are not fully in the light of Christ, certain areas of darkened understanding that need the power of the Word and Spirit to illuminate. The principle to remember, then, is when we are confronted with an area that has become an "idol," remember not to shrink from our duty to attack that area urgently and resolutely. Obedience, keeping a teachable, malleable heart toward the Lord, is one of the great keys to weathering the storms of life. It can be a lot of "work" to keep this hardness toward idolatry, and softness toward the Lord's leadings, but our work *will* be rewarded, so keep at it!

Day 79

"Many are the afflictions of the righteous, but the LORD delivers him out of them all."

Psalm 34:19

*B*eing the righteousness of God in Christ Jesus (2 Corinthians 5:21) does not exclude us from afflictions; in fact, this verse promises we will have many. Jesus never said it was easy to follow Him, only worth it.

Modern day readers usually think of "affliction" as mostly meaning a physical ailment, but the word itself is most properly translated simply "evil" as in the "tree of knowledge of good and evil." (Genesis 2:9) *Ra* (Strong's #H7451) means "unpleasant, disagreeable, wickedness, distress, misery, noisome, calamity, trouble, sorrow, mischief, adversity, vexation." What this book would call the "storms of life." The day-to-day junk, grievances and annoyances we face for taking a stand for righteousness.

David's point in writing this psalm is, "Taste and see that the LORD is good" (Verse 8), which is in direct contrast to the "evils" we find in daily life. Those who "seek the LORD shall not lack any good thing" (Verse 10) in the midst of the "evils" surrounding them. Never forget: "The righteous cry out, and the LORD hears, and delivers them out of all their troubles." (Verse 17)

"Many are the afflictions of the righteous, but the LORD delivers him out of them all."

Psalm 34:19

*G*ood overcomes evil. Eventually good will *remove* evil when Jesus Christ returns, but in the meantime, David's intention is to "teach the fear of the LORD" (Verse 11) for anyone who "desires life" and wants to "see good." (Verse 12) How do we do this? "Keep your tongue from evil, and your lips from speaking deceit. Depart from evil and do good; seek peace and pursue it." (Verses 13-14)

By choosing not to participate in "evil" and choosing to do "good" is the condition for this promise: "the LORD delivers him out of them all." It's not a complicated concept. Be good, don't be evil. But the entire premise of God's deliverance and protection is rooted in the notion of "good *vs.* evil." Black and white. We tend to complicate the issue playing with "shades of gray"—which is often what brings the dreary, gloomy storm clouds our way.

"Little children, keep yourselves from idols. Amen." (1 John 5:21) Do good, refrain from evil, and watch the Lord deliver you from those oppressive storm clouds that want to afflict the righteous so.

❧ Day 81 ❧

"And do not be conformed to this world, but be transformed by the renewing of your mind, that you may prove what is that good and acceptable and perfect will of God."

Romans 12:2

I have heard it taught that there are three levels of God's will—one that is good, one that is acceptable, and one that is perfect, and depending on what "stage" we are in determines how mature we are in God. And in a very limited sense, I can understand this philosophy, that there are stages of growth as we continue to walk toward the perfect will of God. However, strictly speaking, this verse outlines that there is only *one* will, and it is good, acceptable and perfect. We can be in the will of God or out of it (perhaps to a varying degree), even as we continue to grow in our walk with Him onto perfection (or completeness) as Hebrews 6:1 states.

A lot of negative things in this world are attributed to "God's will"—war, famine, sickness, poverty, strife. Since none of these things are "good, acceptable or perfect" to us as flawed humans, they cannot be that way to a perfect God either. We must attribute the storms of life to their proper source (the devil and his corrupt world system), and we must learn how to avoid as much of this system as possible by remaining in that singular will of God.

❧ Day 82 ❧

"And do not be conformed to this world, but be transformed by the renewing of your mind, that you may prove what is that good and acceptable and perfect will of God."

Romans 12:2

So how do we prove this good, acceptable, perfect will of God in our lives, thereby circumventing as much of the "world" and its stormy cycles as we can? *Conform* means "fashion with" (Strong's #G4964, where we get English words like "system" and "scheme")—in other words, don't pattern yourself after the world's patterns: worry, doubt, fear, lust, greed, envy, hatred, violence. *Renewing* speaks of a "complete renovation" (Strong's #G342), a process of sanctification, which means "separation," from the worldly system. This separation is accomplished through the "washing of the water of the Word" (Ephesians 5:26), and by an abiding work of the Holy Spirit's grace given full rein (or *reign*) in our daily lives—see Titus 3:5. When we yield to the Spirit, dying to ourselves daily, He quickens the Word that we read in faith, believing it will change us from the inside out. To the extent we have permitted this to happen is to the extent we are in the singular will of God, and the further in that will we are, the less opportunity the storms of life have to harass us.

❧ *Day 83* ☙

"You will keep him in perfect peace, whose mind is stayed on You, because he trusts in You. Trust in the LORD forever, for in Yah, the LORD, is everlasting strength."

Isaiah 26:3-4

*P*erfect peace" sounds amazing, doesn't it? In the Hebrew, it's actually written "peace peace"—a double promise that conveys absolute certainty into perpetuity, similar to when Jesus says, "Verily, verily." It means "pay attention to this, I've said it twice." This true twice-peace is in opposition to the fake "peace, peace" of false religiosity that "heals" the crushing of the people superficially, as shown in Jeremiah 6:14.

We've alluded elsewhere that the biblical definition of peace does not necessarily mean the absence of all problems and difficulties, but it does mean that Jesus has given us His own peace (John 14:27) in order to view those circumstances through His eyes—that they are subject to change when confronted with the double-peace He offers. In its simplest definition, peace means to have a good journey through life. It's still a journey, but one that can be walked in peace, so long as we keep our minds on the Lord and walk alongside Him every step of the way.

"You will keep him in perfect peace, whose mind is stayed on You, because he trusts in You. Trust in the LORD forever, for in Yah, the LORD, is everlasting strength."

Isaiah 26:3-4

The world's system has two basic ways of dealing with the storms of life: 1) to worry and fret ourselves into exhaustion over them, which produces anger over our own impotence to fix them; or 2) to mentally and emotionally "check out" over them and slip into apathy and mediocrity, being coaxed by the escapism promoted through our media—I mean things like movies, music, entertainment, social media. Now I'm not anti-entertainment, I just mean it only produces a temporary diversion, and when the TV's switched off, we're left with Option 1 to wrestle with in bed all night long. Perfect peace comes from fixating our minds on the Lord as the Solution to our storms. Trust is an important, yet distinct, component of faith. Many well-meaning Christians profess faith in the Lord, but their minds are not fixated on trust in the Lord, so they often fall into the cycle of Options 1 and 2 above. However, the "everlasting strength" to live in "perfect peace" is only found in trusting *forever* the LORD to be true to His Word. If we do that, the storms of life won't rock our boats nearly as much.

"Be anxious for nothing, but in everything by prayer and supplication, with thanksgiving, let your requests be made known to God; and the peace of God, which surpasses all understanding, will guard your hearts and minds through Christ Jesus."

Philippians 4:6-7

*T*he Greek word for *anxious* here comes from a root meaning "distracted, drawn in different directions." (Strong's #G3309) Many times, the storms of life threaten to pull us in all directions, wanting to make us careful (as in "full of care") for the myriad things vying for our attention. While there are certainly physiological and psychological reasons for anxiety that should be treated seriously, this passage provides three keys to keep us being "driven to distraction."

Prayer is simply dialoguing with God, speaking to Him and awaiting His reply—not a one-sided rant, but a conversation, giving the other Party a chance to respond. Supplication is tendering your requests, wants and needs to Him. These are distinct acts yet intertwined. Lastly, thanksgiving is where we get the word *eucharist,* and here means "active gratitude, using grateful language as an act of worship." (Strong's #G2169) Implementing these three components can help us "be anxious for nothing."

❧ Day 86 ❧

"Be anxious for nothing, but in everything by prayer and supplication, with thanksgiving, let your requests be made known to God; and the peace of God, which surpasses all understanding, will guard your hearts and minds through Christ Jesus."

Philippians 4:6-7

Understanding in this passage means what is reasoned or perceived by the intellect. (Strong's #G3563) It speaks of the faculty for rational judgment, the mind. So, in other words, the "peace of God" (that is, God's own peace) goes beyond our human understanding—it is not affected by earthly circumstances, because it is above those circumstances. This passage promises that even during storms, God's peace is granted to you. Peace is defined as: "the tranquil state of a soul assured of its salvation through Christ, and so fearing nothing from God and content with its earthly lot, of whatsoever sort that is." (Strong's #1515)

Guard in this excerpt is a figurative use of a military word meaning "to post a guard or sentinel at a gate," to place an "advance watch" upon one's heart and mind, or "to hem in and protect with a garrison." (Strong's #G5432) The same word is used in 2 Corinthians 11:32 in the literal sense. God's peace mounts a garrison of protection over your heart and mind against outside forces!

"But You, O LORD, are a shield for me, my glory and the One who lifts up my head. I cried to the LORD with my voice, and He heard me from His holy hill. Selah. I lay down and slept; I awoke, for the LORD sustained me. I will not be afraid of ten thousands of people who have set themselves against me all around."

Psalm 3:3-6

S hield in this passage is "buckler," a smaller shield than one that went the entire length of a man. (See Psalm 91:4 for the distinction.) A buckler was strapped to the forearm and could be moved quickly to defend against a flurry of attacks from different angles. The word's root means "to cover over and surround." (Strong's #H4043) As mentioned earlier, it sometimes refers to the scales of a crocodile's hide, implying covering against all angles of attack. (See Job 41:15-17.) Just as a crocodile's thick skin protects him from snout to tail, our God is an impenetrable Shield for us against all attackers, be they circumstances or people. The LORD is our glory— our "shield and exceeding great reward" (Genesis 15:1), our "honor, dignity, splendor, abundant riches." (Strong's #H3519) Because of Him we can face our adversaries, in whatever form they take, with our heads held high, with no fear that He will fail to protect us. In Him, you are a crocodile!

❧ Day 88 ❧

"But You, O LORD, are a shield for me, my glory and the One who lifts up my head. I cried to the LORD with my voice, and He heard me from His holy hill. Selah. I lay down and slept; I awoke, for the LORD sustained me. I will not be afraid of ten thousands of people who have set themselves against me all around."

Psalm 3:3-6

A good night's sleep is an important component of "peace" as the Bible defines it. If peaceful sleep seems superfluous, consider our Lord asleep in the boat when facing an actual "storm of life." (Matthew 8:23-27) And when Jeremiah had a prophetic dream of the restoration and deliverance of Israel, he declared, "...My sleep was sweet to me." (Jeremiah 31:26) In the context of gaining "sound wisdom and discretion," Proverbs 3:24 promises, "When you lie down, you will not be afraid; yes, you will lie down and your sleep will be sweet." David declared, "I will both lie down in peace, and sleep; for You alone, O LORD, make me dwell in safety." (Psalm 4:8) Peaceful sleep cannot be overestimated when faced with difficult circumstances. And you may say, "Easier said than done," when considering all the overwhelming things vying for your attention (and worry) in the night hours. But meditate on Psalm 127 and realize God's role in giving His beloved sleep.

"So Jesus stood still and commanded him to be brought to Him. And when he had come near, He asked him, saying, 'What do you want Me to do for you?'"

Luke 18:40-41

The Lord's question to the blind beggar outside Jericho may seem almost an absurdity. The answer seems abundantly obvious. But the Lord was asking the man to make a claim on his faith in the "Son of David." (Verse 38) Jesus wanted this man to make a decision. Keep in mind the blind man was also a beggar, so not only could he not see, he was destitute because of it.

The first circumstance (blindness) was the root cause of the second (begging.) It seems as if Jesus wanted to find out just how far the man wanted to go with this situation. Did he just want some charity, or something greater? Did the beggar just want to deal with the negative circumstances (poverty), or take care of the root of the issue (blindness)? Of course, the blind man's response was the one Jesus was looking for: Your mercy can fix the root of the problem.

Like the blind beggar, our faith must be active toward the Lord fixing the root issues behind our negative circumstances, not just the circumstances themselves.

❧ Day 90 ☙

"So Jesus stood still and commanded him to be brought to Him. And when he had come near, He asked him, saying, 'What do you want Me to do for you?'"

Luke 18:40-41

Yes, the Lord wants to take care of our needs, but He always wants to open our eyes. The blind beggar symbolizes many people out there: those who are spiritually blind *and* dirt poor. Many of us cry out to the Lord for mercy, wanting our most immediate need taken care of, which isn't wrong; but often we neglect the deeper reasons for that immediate need. It's like the well-known proverb: "Give a man a fish, feed him for a day; teach a man to fish, feed him for life." God wants us to ask that He open our eyes, spiritually speaking, to understand more deeply His work of mercy. And out of that enlightenment will come the provision for our needs.

We, too, need to ask in faith, "Lord, that I may receive my sight." (See Ephesians 1:18-20.) Once our faith has made us well (Verse 42), our response needs to be "glorifying God." But notice, it's not just *our* response to God's mercy, the people around us will give praise to God. (Verse 43) Their "eyes" will be opened too. The mercy of God responding to faith creates a ripple effect.

"Therefore, my beloved brethren, be steadfast, immovable, always abounding in the work of the LORD, knowing that your labor is not in vain in the LORD."

1 Corinthians 15:58

Steadfast in this passage comes from the Greek verb meaning "to sit." (Strong's #G1476) In modern speech it would convey the idea of "sitting sedentary," being deskbound, immobile. Similarly, *immovable* metaphorically means the opposite of moving away to another location, remaining where we are. (Strong's #G3334) We are instructed by Paul to be entirely unshaken in our knowledge that laboring for the Lord will produce a reward from Him. "Abounding in the work of the LORD" speaks of going above and beyond, to exceed expectations and excel above the regular measure. (Strong's #G4052) *Ergo* is the Greek word for "work" (Strong's #G2041), and it encompasses all kinds of work, any "product, enterprise, undertaking, industry or art."

"And whatever you do, do it heartily, as to the LORD and not to men…" (Colossians 3:23) Often our storms of life come from outside sources, work, family, friends, as opposed to internal conflict. One of the ways to find shelter from these external storms is by "working for the LORD," instead of for ourselves or others.

❧ Day 92 ☙

"Therefore, my beloved brethren, be steadfast, immovable, always abounding in the work of the LORD, knowing that your labor is not in vain in the LORD."

1 Corinthians 15:58

Labor in this passage is a separate word from "work." It is literally "a beating of the breast with grief or sorrow." (Strong's #G2873) Things that make "more work for us" or "cause us trouble." The word signifies intensity in toiling against something.

When our work and labor are coupled with the faith and understanding that we do these things unto the Lord, we're assured that what we are doing is effective and will produce a positive result. We undergo adversity and hard work *for* Him, because we love Him and trust Him that our "labor is not in vain." Not unto others, or for ourselves, or for work's sake—it is all to be for Him, and this implies there is work and labor that is *not* for Him and, therefore, ultimately vain. That word means "empty" (Strong's #G2756), pointless, fruitless. Our daily work and the labors we face must be for the Lord's sake in order to create lasting value—otherwise, we undergo difficulties and strive against them without producing fruit. We all will face storms in life; let's ensure they *mean* something unto the Lord. We will not have struggled in vain.

❧ *Day 93* ❧

"Then Joshua said to them, 'Do not be afraid, nor be dismayed; be strong and of good courage, for thus the LORD will do to all your enemies against whom you fight.'"

Joshua 10:25

When we work and labor for the Lord's sake, we are assured the Lord's victory in our circumstances. The reason the Israelites were successful in conquering the Promised Land was because they had been instructed by Him how and when to invade.

When we feel we are consistently hitting a wall against a certain obstacle or undertaken endeavor, we need to back up and pause to listen to instruction from God. Is this just normal adversity we're to plow through, or are we doing something in vain; that is, "not unto the Lord"?

It is the Holy Spirit's responsibility to reveal truth (John 16:13), and it is that truth, once we know it, that makes us free. (John 8:32) Free in this instance means "victorious against our adverse circumstances." However, we have the responsibility of waiting in expectation, hope and faith, upon the Spirit, then being obedient to that revealed truth and not operate outside of its direction.

❧ Day 94 ❧

"Then Joshua said to them, 'Do not be afraid, nor be dismayed; be strong and of good courage, for thus the LORD will do to all your enemies against whom you fight.'"

Joshua 10:25

Fear is a major hindrance to the truth of the Spirit being fruitful and victorious in our lives. You have most likely heard many sermons against fear, but of course, it's easier to say "fear not" than to be actually fearless. However, this is not a valid excuse for being fearful. The Bible teaches, "There is no fear in love; but perfect love casts out fear, because fear involves torment. But he who fears has not been made perfect in love. We love Him because He first loved us." (1 John 4:18-19) If we still have fear, does that mean we're failures? No, it just means we have not been made perfect in love—it is a lifestyle process of growing in love with the One who first loved us. There is no excuse to remain ignorant of God's love when faced with adversaries.

Dismayed here literally means "to be shattered, broken" (Strong's #H2865) by terror. Giving into fear in light of the level of perfection we have received in God's love causes us to be splintered and traumatized by the storms of life. We must continue to grow in our understanding of God's love in order to be kept whole.

❧ *Day 95* ❦

"In this you greatly rejoice, though now for a little while, if need be, you have been grieved by various trials, that the genuineness of your faith, being much more precious than gold that perishes, though it is tested by fire, may be found to praise, honor, and glory at the revelation of Jesus Christ..."

1 Peter 1:6-7

G reatly rejoice" refers to the previous verse: being "kept by the power of God." (Verse 5) But Peter goes on to say we may be grieved for a little while by various trials. "A little while" is how we render the Greek word *oligos* (Strong's #G3641) which means "few, little, small, slight or short." It is my conviction that God never intended for us to be under a relentless barrage of the storms of life. That's not to say we won't have them, but I do not believe God wants us to live miserable lives that are constantly under attack.

This shows me that there is a higher place in being "kept by God" where these life struggles become fewer and further between. It is God's ultimate objective that we grow in relationship with Him where we are "kept" from constant onslaught. This relationship is grown over time out of obedience and love as we repent from dead works and turn our faith toward Him. (See Hebrews 6:1.)

❧ Day 96 ❧

"In this you greatly rejoice, though now for a little while, if need be, you have been grieved by various trials, that the genuineness of your faith, being much more precious than gold that perishes, though it is tested by fire, may be found to praise, honor, and glory at the revelation of Jesus Christ..."

1 Peter 1:6-7

*V*arious trials" is "manifold temptations" in the original King James. It speaks of "proving" (Strong's #G3986) one's fidelity; that is, the "genuineness of your faith" through a trial by fire. A lot of incorrect theology stems from a veiled understanding of *why* God allows our faith to be tried by the storms of life. Natural creation operates under the tenet that there is no growth without resistance. Stagnation produces unproductivity.

Since God cannot grow or change, then the principle of resistance training applies to us. It is not for His benefit that you are tried and refined. God is not trying to squeeze you "just because." Your proper response to the adversities in this life will bring "praise, honor and glory"—not only to God—but to *you* when the Lord returns and rewards each of us according to what we've done. (See Revelation 22:12.) Do not shirk the refining fire—recognize it is for your benefit!

❧ *Day 97* ❧

"Come to Me, all you who labor and are heavy laden, and I will give you rest. Take My yoke upon you and learn from Me, for I am gentle and lowly in heart, and you will find rest for your souls. For My yoke is easy and My burden is light."

Matthew 11:28-30

"*C*ome to me" in the Greek is imperative. It could be rendered, "Come now!" This command is given by Jesus in context of Him previously declaring He is the only Way by which the Father may be known. (Verse 27) John 6:35-40 shows that "coming to Jesus" is more than a casual, chance meeting (the people to whom He was speaking had already gathered to hear Him)—it really means "believe in Me!" That is a condition for receiving the "rest" He promises to give.

The word *labor* is speaking of grief, to "grow exhausted with toil or burden." (Strong's #G2872) As we showed in a previous entry, it is a derivative of the word meaning "to beat one's breast with grief and sorrow."

The Lord is declaring here, "You can trade your grief and sorrow for My yoke, which is easier to bear." If you believe in Him, if you genuinely love Him and keep His commandments (John 14:15), the rest from your wearisome griefs and sorrows can be your portion. What a gift!

❧ *Day 98* ❧

"Come to Me, all you who labor and are heavy laden, and I will give you rest. Take My yoke upon you and learn from Me, for I am gentle and lowly in heart, and you will find rest for your souls. For My yoke is easy and My burden is light."

Matthew 11:28-30

*H*eavy laden" is speaking to people who are sensible to their burden of toiling for God's acceptance and are looking for a Way out of their circumstances; it isn't speaking of people who are indifferent to their plight in sin and adversity. Sadly, many people are defined by their misery and remain apathetic toward anything that could change their circumstances. In order to receive the "rest" Christ promises, we must want to accept His offer and actively pursue it—it doesn't happen automatically. (See Hebrews 11:6.)

The phrase "heavy laden" is speaking of "spiritual anxiety," being overburdened with religious ceremonies and formalities—the Law, which can never be attained by human power. (Strong's #G5412) Christ completes the Law for us (Matthew 5:17), and we enter the fulfillment of that Law by our faith in Him. You cannot overcome the storms of life under your own strength—it requires the completed work of Jesus in your stead.

❧ Day 99 ❧

"The LORD bless you and keep you; the LORD make His face shine upon you, and be gracious to you; the LORD lift up His countenance upon you, and give you peace."

Numbers 6:24-26

The Aaronic blessing has been a source of comfort to Jews and Christians alike for millennia. While we don't place emphasis on the liturgical or formulaic elements of the words themselves, like some magical chant, the LORD's blessing is a powerful and true spiritual precept. Where would we be without God's blessing upon us? The storms of life would surely overwhelm us!

Keep properly means to "hedge about as with thorns." (Strong's #H8104) To preserve and protect as a watchman keeps his charge. Blessing in the Hebrew conveys the notion of "bending the knees;" that is, kneeling. (Strong's #H1288) Our normal context would be *us* blessing the LORD, kneeling before Him; but the concept goes both ways. Here we envision the LORD Himself, God of all creation, deigning to stoop down from His lofty position so that He might bless us. When applied personally, this truth is simply overwhelming.

The extreme honor of being blessed by the LORD keeps us sheltered from the storms we face.

❧ Day 100 ❦

"The LORD bless you and keep you; the LORD make His face shine upon you, and be gracious to you; the LORD lift up His countenance upon you, and give you peace."

Numbers 6:24-26

*M*ake His face shine…" is such an amazing visual. By implication, "face" means to turn and look upon you, to cause His presence to rest upon you. (Strong's #H6437 and #H6440) To regard you personally, individually. "Shine" means "to become bright," (Strong's #H215) and Gesenius points out it is the same word "enlightened" in 1 Samuel 14:27,29: "used of the eyes of a faint person when he begins to recover."

The LORD God has condescended to "lift up His countenance" upon you to bestow the blessing of peace and be gracious to you. Gracious means "to show favor and have pity." (Strong's #H2603)

Whenever you are faced with a difficult trial in life, keep this blessing in the forefront of your thinking. Because you have chosen to pursue the Lord wholeheartedly, you have caught His attention and He has turned His face upon you with grace and blessing. Just as when God turned to consider Mary, we too are "blessed" and "highly favored" (Luke 1:28) when we pursue righteousness. (See Matthew 5:6.)

❧ Day 101 ❧

"Hope deferred makes the heart sick, but when the desire comes, it is a tree of life."

Proverbs 13:12

*H*ope is a vital component of faith; they go hand-in-hand. The word itself in the Hebrew comes from a root that conveys "waiting in expectancy, tarrying." (Strong's #H3176) Oftentimes I see people confuse faith and hope. While they are complementary, the foundation of hope is faith, not the other way 'round. (Hebrews 11:1) Faith is something accepted as being true "now," while hope looks to future fulfilment. Faith feeds hope, but hope keeps faith fresh and active, engaged. Biblical hope cannot come if it is not rooted in faith. We are saved by faith *now* (Ephesians 2:8-9), but we look with hope to our faith's future consummation at Christ's Second Coming. (Titus 2:13) Faith is a present reality based upon actual past occurrences (i.e., we are saved today because we believe and confess Christ died for our sins, and was raised from the dead, in the past—Romans 10:9.) Faith is assured and settled; hope is always future tense, otherwise there is no need for hope. (Romans 8:24) When seeking shelter from the storms of life, make sure your expectancy (hope of deliverance) is based in the faith that God has *already* won your victory. (1 John 5:4)

☙ Day 102 ❧

"Hope deferred makes the heart sick, but when the desire comes, it is a tree of life."

Proverbs 13:12

*D*eferred hope can feel like a prolonged illness; it can literally hurt our hearts, but many people only focus on the first part of this verse. The point of this proverb is not that hope is deferred (so feel bad), but rather hope's fulfilment (desire) *will* come; and when it does, it's like a tree of life (so feel good.) The assurance by faith that our desires will be fulfilled keeps deferred hope from turning toxic.

The ultimate expression of hope abiding in faith is love. (1 Corinthians 13:13) This verse is often presented as a linear progression: faith creates hope creates love, and I see where this concept comes from; but we need to remember that *all three* abide (remain), all are vital, so instead of linear, it's cyclical. Love being the greatest does not demean faith and hope. Rather, according to 1 Corinthians 13:4-8, love defines hope fed by faith. Love is longsuffering and never fails, so it is the united work of faith and hope in action. Our faith is assured of hope's desire because of God's love for us. As we return that love to Him, it keeps hope alive and allows faith's spiritual truth to manifest in our natural reality.

"And you would be secure, because there is hope; yes, you would dig around you, and take your rest in safety. You would also lie down, and no one would make you afraid; yes, many would court your favor."

Job 11:18-19

*S*ecure in this passage means "to confide one's trust, hope and confidence in another, to make bold, secure." (Strong's #H982) If we put our trust in God and follow His commandments (Verses 13-14) we forget our misery (Verse 16) and then "there is hope." Recall that *hope* is a "cord" that attaches us to God. It binds us to Him, but it is contingent upon our faith and obedience to Him. Many people profess faith in God, but do not feel "secure" in Him—they question the trust and hope they put in Him.

Like Job, for most people, this isn't because of wanton rebellion—they genuinely want to believe God is trustworthy, but their life experiences have taught them that as people will eventually fail them, how is God any different?

It can sometimes feel like a scary step to walk blindly after God, having no worry for tomorrow (Matthew 6:34), trusting in His integrity—but this is an essential truth of finding shelter from the storms. Trust Him for security!

❧ Day 104 ❧

"And you would be secure, because there is hope; yes, you would dig around you, and take your rest in safety. You would also lie down, and no one would make you afraid; yes, many would court your favor."

Job 11:18-19

*E*veryone is looking for security, but most often it is misplaced in people or human institutions, which ultimately will fail. To "rest in safety" requires us to search out the Source of security—the Lord Jesus Christ. The word *dig* here implies "searching out or seeking" (Strong's #H2658)—pursuing Him who would make us safe. Once we have found Him, we would *lie down* and be unafraid. The phrase here speaks of reposing like a quadruped animal rests, with the legs tucked underneath them, resting on their breast, the picture of total security. (Strong's #H7257) The word *afraid* is also more poetic in the Hebrew: "to shudder or tremble with terror, like a mountain quakes." (Strong's #H2729)

This type of peace and security is attractive to the world at large. When they see we are unmoved by the storms of life, they inquire of us, "What's our Secret?" The phrase implies one being "sick, wounded, weak, grieved, rubbed or worn down" (Strong's #H2470) and thus entreating us to share the Remedy we have found. They will "court our favor."

❧ Day 105 ❧

"The Lord takes pleasure in those who fear Him, in those who hope in His mercy."

Psalm 147:11

*F*ear in this passage must be taken in context with the rest of the verse. Many people think that God is angry with them and subsequently, they fear His retaliation, that He is "up there" just looking for someone who steps out of line so He can hit that SMITE button. It is equally true that God is both wrathful and loving. (Romans 1:18-23; John 3:16) However, the wrath of God must be viewed in balance with His love, and vice versa. Just like you are capable of great anger and great compassion, so is your Lord.

So yes, fear here means "fear," but it comes from a root meaning "to honor, reverence, awe, dread." (Strong's #H3373) It is a fear that produces veneration and a desire to be holy as God is holy. (1 Peter 1:16) There *is* such a thing as healthy fear. And yet that fear of the Lord must always be defined in the context of our love of Him. If fear is misplaced, it prolongs the negative circumstances in our lives by mislaying dread upon the wrong things—the circumstances that change. God is unchanging, and just as our fear of Him should never vary, neither should our understanding that it is His unwavering love that delivers us!

"The LORD takes pleasure in those who fear Him, in those who hope in His mercy."

Psalm 147:11

*J*ust as the LORD finds pleasure in those who fear Him, He equally finds pleasure in those who hope in His mercy. Misconstruing His love is just as dangerous as misconstruing His holiness. Not putting our hope in Him can be just as sinful as out-and-out rebelling against His decrees. Many sincere Christians take great care to keep from sinning against God outwardly, but do not consider their misplaced fear in the storms of life, or their lack of trust and hope in Him for deliverance, as equally errant. God's mercy cannot be separated from His holiness—without the one, He does not have the other. It is *because* of His great holiness that He procured the means of obtaining His mercy through Jesus's atoning sacrifice. Dismissing one or the other is likewise dismissive of Jesus's work on the cross. Christ died so that we might obtain mercy through His holiness infused within us by the sanctifying work of the Holy Spirit. It is the only way to have proper fear, and therefore, the only way to have mercy. When faced with trials, never forget—fear the Lord only and place all your hope in His mercy that the Kingdom of Heaven is, indeed, near unto you. (Luke 10:9)

❧ *Day 107* ❧

"Therefore humble yourselves under the mighty hand of God, that He may exalt you in due time, casting all your care upon Him, for He cares for you."

1 Peter 5:6-7

*M*ost every Christian is familiar with this verse. I'm sure nearly all of us have quoted "cast all your care upon Him because He cares for you!" There is another component to this wonderfully comforting verse: "humble yourselves." The truth of casting your cares upon Him is very real, but it is also very self-effacing to admit you need Someone else to carry your burdens for you. This is where many Christians struggle. They seek the blessings of God apart from the humility that is required to receive them. All of us are guilty of being less than humble from time-to-time; I cannot be the only one.

The literal meaning of the Greek verb for *humble* is "to level to a plain." (Strong's #G5013) That provides an apt image for what God considers humility. We must learn not to raise ourselves up but wait for the Lord to exalt us. To the extent we have surrendered humbly before God is the extent to which we can truly cast our cares upon Him and be content in waiting for Him to raise us from the plain to the mountaintop.

❧ *Day 108* ❧

"Therefore humble yourselves under the mighty hand of God, that He may exalt you in due time, casting all your care upon Him, for He cares for you."

1 Peter 5:6-7

*F*or He cares for you" is proof that God is not far from our plight. (Acts 17:27) He is not distantly removed from our situation. Psalm 55:22 says, "Cast your burden on the Lord, and He shall sustain you; He shall never permit the righteous to be moved." The marginalia for *moved* shows "shaken." You *can* live a life unshaken by storms when you come into the truth that by humbling yourself under His hand, you can roll those storms off on Him, expecting God to raise you above them in due time. The word for *hand* (Strong's #G5495) here stems from roots that mean a "channel for power" to flow through, "upholding and preserving" the one who receives that power. Literally, a "chasm" that receives "pouring rain." Humbling ourselves under that cascading flow will cause us to be raised up in *due time.* That phrase is *kairos* (Strong's #2540), the "opportune time" or "right season." It may take some time after casting our cares before we see that we are lifted off the plain and into the mountaintop—but we can be assured God *will* as we humble ourselves under His mighty hand.

❧ Day 109 ❧

"The LORD sat enthroned at the Flood, and the LORD sits as King forever. The LORD will give strength to His people; the LORD will bless His people with peace."

Psalm 29:10-11

In every other instance in the Old Testament, the word for "Flood" (Strong's #H3999) used here means the deluge that occurred in Noah's time (see Genesis 6-8), so that is why it's capitalized in the NKJV. However, many theologians admit a possible exception to the instance used in Psalm 29:10. While I'm not dogmatic either way, I think it's a wonderfully comforting thought that God sits as King forever, even over the "floods" we face in life. The point here is that God *was* King then and God *will be* King forever.

Even during the worst moments of our lives, we can take solace that God is, indeed, King over all—and if we trust in His goodness and mercy, we *will* weather the storms. This doesn't mean we like going through storms, but it does mean His trustworthiness will ensure we are preserved and blessed through them. The storms, like the Flood, will eventually subside. Take heart! As King, God watches over His loyal subjects to make certain they are carried over the floodwaters and rise to the top victorious.

✥ Day 110 ✥

"The LORD sat enthroned at the Flood, and the LORD sits as King forever. The LORD will give strength to His people; the LORD will bless His people with peace."

Psalm 29:10-11

While all of the spiritual gifts and fruit in a Spirit-filled Christian's life are equally important, especially at specific times of need, surely *strength* and *peace* are among the most vitally valuable in day-to-day activities. The "little storms" of daily life can drain us and wear us down to the point that when "major storms" roll in, we feel utterly ill-equipped to deal with them.

The key, then, is to keep pulling upon the strength and peace that the King offers His people consistently. These are limitless commodities made available to us because they come from the Lord's inexhaustible storehouse: Himself. They are byproducts of His existence as King forever. Because God Is Peace (Judges 6:24), we have His peace. Because God Is Victor (Exodus 15:17), we have His strength. He imparts them to you to the level you submit to His wisdom, align your lifestyle to the directives established by His Word, and trust in His faithfulness. Ultimately these attributes are rooted in His love for us. (Song of Solomon 2:4) If we give Him all of us, we get all of Him, and no flood can drown us!

✥ Day 111 ✥

"I will hear what God the LORD will speak, for He will speak peace to His people and to His saints; but let them not turn back to folly. Surely His salvation is near to those who fear Him, that glory may dwell in our land. Mercy and truth have met together; righteousness and peace have kissed."

Psalm 85:8-10

Folly means "foolishness, silliness, stupidity." (Strong's #H3690) Not necessarily egregious sin (although that's certainly included in "foolish") but rather an overreliance on our own conventions and wisdom, strength and power. The word comes from a root meaning "flanks, loins," or the lower part of the back (above the kidneys) that is the source of strength. (See Proverbs 31:17.) More properly it means "to be fat"—it's the word used for the fat surrounding the viscera in Leviticus 3. This fat was burned upon the altar and not eaten by the priests (Verse 17) because all the "fat" (strength) is the Lord's. (Verse 16) While the visual is a bit gross, the point here is to show that God's people, when they do not listen to Him speaking, are being foolish, even stupid, relying on their own "fatness." (See Jeremiah 10:8—same word.) Don't return to folly; let God's "fatness" lead you!

❦ Day 112 ❦

"I will hear what God the LORD will speak, for He will speak peace to His people and to His saints; but let them not turn back to folly. Surely His salvation is near to those who fear Him, that glory may dwell in our land. Mercy and truth have met together; righteousness and peace have kissed."

Psalm 85:8-10

*M*ercy and truth, righteousness and peace, are merged together in the salvation of the Lord. Salvation is an all-inclusive word (where we get the name "Jesus"): "safety, welfare, prosperity, victory." (Strong's #H3468) Not just for the afterlife, but so that "glory may dwell in our land" in *this* life. Sure, the land may have storms sometimes, but God "rescues" those who fear Him. *Mercy* (Strong's #H2617) can be translated "favor, goodness, kindness." It is the boon companion of *truth* (Strong's #H571), which can be rendered "reliability or stability, firmness, sureness, faithfulness." These two attributes of God are eternally linked: there is truth because of mercy, and vice versa, the same for righteousness and peace. *Righteousness* (Strong's #H6664) means "justice." The word *kissed* (Strong's #H5401) is also used for equipping with a weapon, to arm, akin to strengthen or kindle, overlay or adhere together. These four traits go hand-in-hand with God's salvation.

⊰ *Day 113* ⊱

"For the mountains shall depart and the hills be removed, but My kindness shall not depart from you, nor shall My covenant of peace be removed,' says the LORD, who has mercy on you."

Isaiah 54:10

Kindness, such as the Lord possesses, is more than simple gesture or sentiment. Our concept of kindness is often described as "being nice," perhaps an act of charity or sympathy. Kindness is those things, but as an attribute of God Himself, it is much deeper. It is something that motivates and drives Him. Recall from earlier that the word conveys an intense desire, ardor, zeal, eagerness. Actively seeking out someone to bestow His kindness upon. It is a wrong notion, unsupported by Scripture, that God remains aloof while enthroned in heaven, enshrouded in clouds, virtually indifferent to what happens down here on earth. While I try to maintain a balance theologically between God's holiness (separateness) and His nearness, it's been my experience that more people view God as alienated, or being at odds with them, or even antagonistic and openly hostile toward His creation. The truth is, even if the earth itself is "removed," His kindness toward us remains forever, not in a passive, dismissive feeling, but actively engaged in benevolence and compassion.

✥ Day 114 ✥

"For the mountains shall depart and the hills be removed, but My kindness shall not depart from you, nor shall My covenant of peace be removed,' says the LORD, who has mercy on you."

Isaiah 54:10

God is quick to forgive (Ephesians 4:32; 1 John 1:9), slow to anger (Psalm 103:8), rich in mercy. (Ephesians 2:4) The biblical concept of God's mercy shows His clemency in *withholding* judgment against those who are deserving of it. The perception that God is looking to punish people is fallacy. Yes, God is holy and demands holiness (1 Peter 1:16), but He has already placed judgment upon our sin through the crucifixion of Christ and broken its power over us by raising Him from the dead. Nothing you ever do, good or bad, is going to surprise Him. All that remains is for you to accept that kindness, endeavoring to live a lifestyle that is pleasing in His sight (1 John 3:22) and, when you fail in that pursuit, to be honest with Him in needing His mercy. He *will* give it.

That is the "covenant of peace" that is promised to His people. A covenant is a binding, eternal pledge, a blood oath, between two parties to share all their resources with the other. We categorically come out on top in this agreement!

᚛ᚐ *Day 115* ᚐ᚜

"For you shall go out with joy, and be led out with peace; the mountains and the hills shall break forth into singing before you, and all the trees of the field shall clap their hands."

Isaiah 55:12

Joy and peace, two of the most wonderful effects of walking with the Lord in this life, are stated immediately after the very famous Verse 11: "So shall My word be that goes forth from My mouth; it shall not return to Me void, but it shall accomplish what I please, and it shall prosper in the thing for which I sent it." *Void* means "empty, fruitless." The promises of God, joy and peace, are not empty. His Words inherently contain the power to make what He is saying actualized in this present, natural earth you and I live on. We are not talking about "joy and peace" in the distant future, or some other plane of existence, but in the here and now.

This doesn't mean we have joy and peace instantly, in every circumstance. There is a working through time to make these promises operational. They do not occur by happenstance, but by appropriating through faith God's kindness, that He means what He says; and by lining up our lives with those Words, we receive the promise of joy and peace no matter what storms are raging around us.

☙ Day 116 ❧

"For you shall go out with joy, and be led out with peace; the mountains and the hills shall break forth into singing before you, and all the trees of the field shall clap their hands."

Isaiah 55:12

*G*o out" and "led out" are two different words. One implies self-action, getting up and going out; the other implies being carried or borne along. (Strong's #H2986) Gesenius states this word most properly conveys "to flow, especially copiously and with some violence, like a rain shower." These two words describe dual activity, where we work with God to go out ourselves and be carried along swiftly by Him. Joy and peace are things we must work for. "Let him turn away from evil and do good; let him seek peace and pursue it." (1 Peter 3:11) Romans 14:17 tells us the kingdom of God is "righteousness, peace and joy in the Holy Spirit." That shows a progression, a life-pursuit. We cannot earn righteousness. That is imputed by faith in Christ, yielding peace and its counterpart, joy, which we are instructed to pursue with violence (that is, "great activity, intensity and ferocity"—not cruelty or brutality.) "And from the days of John the Baptist until now the kingdom of heaven suffers violence, and the violent take it by force." (Matthew 11:12) Be forceful in appropriating joy and peace!

> *Day 117* <<

*"These things I have spoken to you, that in Me you may have peace.
In the world you will have tribulation; but be of good cheer, I have
overcome the world."*

John 16:33

Tribulation sounds like such a gloomy word. Nobody wants tribulation; unfortunately we'll all get it. In the Greek (Strong's #G2347), it conveys the concept of being squeezed, like how a grape is pressed to make wine. I've mentioned earlier I don't think "tribulation" means we have to accept life-threatening illnesses, but the word means "affliction" in the context of burdens, hardships, troubles, persecutions, distresses—all those storms of life that result in making a stand for Christ. Being "in the world" while following Jesus will invariably create pressure since the world system is opposed to sound Christian doctrine that Jesus is Lord. Even for the privileged Christians in Western society, it is becoming more and more "pressing" to follow Him. And that's okay; pursuing something worthwhile is never easy, and our faith in the Lord is the most worthwhile thing! Jesus doesn't pull any punches: you're going to be squeezed by the world, but take heart, because He *has already* overcome the world. We can be comforted by the biblical truth that the difficult pursuit of a godly lifestyle brings the greatest of rewards.

⚘ *Day 118* ⚘

"These things I have spoken to you, that in Me you may have peace. In the world you will have tribulation; but be of good cheer, I have overcome the world."

John 16:33

C *heer* is the opposite of a gloomy word. Everybody wants to be cheerful. In the New Testament, the Greek word (Strong's #G2293) is always in the imperative, meaning it's intended as a command: be comforted! Like a general would tell his soldiers, "Take courage, lads!" *Good cheer* is akin to the word meaning "confidence, boldness, daring."

So when we're faced with tribulation, we are to respond with courage and cheer. It is a decision we make, to respond positively to the Lord's command, or to disobey. That doesn't mean we *enjoy* being squeezed by the storms of life, but it does mean we have a choice on how we respond to those pressures. I understand that mental health can play a role in making that decision, so it's "easier said than done" for those who struggle with clinical depression or a similar malady. I'm not treating those legitimate issues flippantly. However, it doesn't negate the overall truth that *in Christ*, you will overcome the world, because He has already done so. Our persuasion must be firm to "be of good cheer" even during tribulation.

Day 119

"Now may the Lord of peace Himself give you peace always in every way. The Lord be with you all."

2 Thessalonians 3:16

"Prince of peace" is a title given to the Lord Jesus Christ from Old Testament times. (Isaiah 9:6) He is not only the Possessor of peace, being peaceable Himself, but also the Originator of peace, meaning all peace comes from Him. Without Him, there is no true, lasting peace. Further, *Prince* means "ruler, governor, chief." (Strong's #H8269) So as the Leader of peace, He demands peace from His loyal subjects. We must seek out peace. "If it is possible, as much as depends on you, live peaceably with all men." (Romans 12:18)

If we accept that a sizeable portion of the storms we face are in our purview to control—meaning our actions *create* our stormy situations, at least sometimes—we must also accept that keeping peace, as much as it is contingent upon our activity, is a commandment from the Lord. Recall 1 Peter 3:11; we are told to pursue peace. Many Christians ask for peace from the Lord, not understanding that peace, at least in certain circumstances, is something they pursue in obedience to God's commandment as Prince of peace. Be sure to seek peace with all the relationships in your power. That just may prevent a lot of storms from coming your way!

❧ Day 120 ❧

"Now may the Lord of peace Himself give you peace always in every way. The Lord be with you all."

2 Thessalonians 3:16

For those times when it's *not* in our power to sue for peace, Paul's faith-filled prayer here is for the Lord to give you that peace "always in every way." Really, even when peace is within our domain, it's the Lord who is giving us the peace, since it all stems from Him. But the context of this benediction is Paul's discourse on "disorderly" and "idle" brethren, "busybodies." If Paul warns us not to keep company with such people (not as an enemy, but to admonish them as brothers), he certainly intends we should not be disorderly, idle busybodies ourselves! Do not be a disturber of the peace!

"In every way" is sometimes translated "in every place." This covers the entire gamut of "giving peace." At all times, in every method, condition, and action, in every physical location and circumstance. That pretty much covers "always and every."

How is this peace given? "The Lord be with you all." His abiding presence, which is an act of grace, coupled with our cooperation with the direction of His Spirit in all the circumstances of life will keep us in peace. That sounds like a great way to live!

❧ *Day 121* ❧

"Now may the God of hope fill you with all joy and peace in believing, that you may abound in hope by the power of the Holy Spirit."

Romans 15:13

Like the title *Prince of peace*, "God of hope" implies ownership, rulership—He is the Source of hope, and true, biblical hope originates in Him. There is a worldly type of hope, just as there is a worldly type of peace and joy, but these originate by mankind's efforts, a pale reflection of God's hope, peace and joy. They are fleeting and cannot remain permanently, since they are based in impermanent, earthly circumstances. Worldly hope, peace and joy are not *evil*; they just fall woefully short of being able to impart a lasting effect, which is why people are always looking for new sources of hope, peace and joy. When that earthly source dries up, people are left with a cyclical emotional response: hope becomes despair, peace becomes turmoil, joy becomes sorrow, and they are forced to look for other sources.

When our hope, peace and joy are rooted in God, the Source can never be exhausted. It is still a pursuit on our part to keep plugged into that Source, but that pursuit breaks the cycle of emotional upheaval, even when external storms loom on the horizon. It's simply a better way!

❧ *Day 122* ❧

"Now may the God of hope fill you with all joy and peace in believing, that you may abound in hope by the power of the Holy Spirit."

Romans 15:13

*H*ope which is rooted in God produces joy and peace. However, this is not automatic. Notice Paul says, "in believing." There is an exercise of faith in that hope which generates joy and peace. It's "faith, hope, love" which abide according to 1 Corinthians 13:13—the order here can show a progression. The above passage states that we "abound in hope" by the "power of the Holy Spirit." He responds to our faith by granting power. This is true of all spiritual gifts—salvation occurs when faith is given, producing power for regeneration of the human spirit. Faith is exercised during the baptism of the Holy Spirit, and power is generated, expressed in the release of a heavenly prayer language.

Faith in the "God of hope" produces the Holy Spirit's power, which is manifested in "all joy and peace." The verb "fill" implies a progression, a process of increasing hope, joy and peace as faith is put in. This is still a cycle, like the worldly pursuit of these things; but because the Source is infinite, the progressive "filling" is never-ending. Believing in faith is the best expenditure of energy you can make!

❧ Day 123 ❦

"Have you not known? Have you not heard? The everlasting God, the LORD, the Creator of the ends of the earth, neither faints nor is weary. His understanding is unsearchable. He gives power to the weak, and to those who have no might He increases strength."

Isaiah 40:28-29

I think these questions in Isaiah are great proofs that a relationship with God is to be experienced through the five senses, tangibly on the earthly plane. Each question here is a single word in the Hebrew. "Have you not known?" is "to ascertain by seeing." (Strong's #H3045) It's the same word used in Genesis 3:5. "Have you not heard?" is "to perceive by the ear with attention or interest." (Strong's #H8085) I am convinced that to believe God exists, to put your faith in Him for salvation and not experience that truth in the here and now is very far below God's expectations for His people. To me, it demeans His existence as "God, the LORD, the Creator..." to be only experienced when we die. That cheapens the entire point of existence upon the earth—what is life for, if we only experience God after we've left it? Many Christians seem to have this expectation, that experiencing God only happens when they die. That forces them to live within the storms of life without any true hope, joy, peace, etc. It's a weak way to live!

❧ Day 124 ❧

"Have you not known? Have you not heard? The everlasting God, the LORD, the Creator of the ends of the earth, neither faints nor is weary. His understanding is unsearchable. He gives power to the weak, and to those who have no might He increases strength."

Isaiah 40:28-29

*E*verlasting comes from the root for "hidden, concealed"— the "vanishing point" on the horizon. (Strong's #H5769) It speaks of time out of mind and future into perpetuity. Our God is a never-ending Source of divine energy, never fatiguing, never exhausting. His strength is so limitless that we are incapable of discovering the ends of His abilities. That phrase "His understanding is unsearchable" not only speaks of His intelligence, but also His consideration and regard for us. There is no end to it.

He is uniquely qualified to "understand" our weakness and out of His infinite power, He increases ours. When things don't turn out the way we expected, or we don't see an immediate answer to our circumstances, God "increases strength" to us in the interim. Our hope in faith is refreshed, our concept of His unlimited understanding is enlarged, we are renewed even in the midst of great activity and stress. We are carried through the storm!

❧ Day 125 ❧

"My soul clings to the dust; revive me according to Your word. My soul melts from heaviness; strengthen me according to Your word."

Psalm 119:25,28

*P*salm 119 is the longest chapter in the Bible and one of my personal favorites for meditation and reflection. I think it was written by King David, though some scholars suggest Ezra or Daniel. But to me, the phraseology and thematic construction (it's an acrostic) point to Davidian authorship.

Dust in this passage is analogous to ashes, "to be grey." (Strong's #H6083) It can speak of burning rubbish reduced to powder. (See Nehemiah 4.) Here the psalmist equates his soulish state (his mind, will and emotions) has been ground down, pulverized, into ash. It conveys the image of being virtually destroyed, turned into something unrecognizable, by his circumstances. Can we relate to this visual sometimes?

The psalmist relies upon God's *word*—His decree, commandment (Strong's #H1697)—to revive him. The same word is used in Genesis 18:14: "Is anything too hard for the Lord?" *Revive* (Strong's #H2421) means "preserve, quicken, sustain, restore." God's word brings us out of the ashes and reconditions our souls!

❧ Day 126 ❧

"My soul clings to the dust; revive me according to Your word. My soul melts from heaviness; strengthen me according to Your word."

Psalm 119:25,28

*M*elts (Strong's #H1811) is probably better conveyed by "drops," as how rain drips through holes in a roof. It communicates "weeping steadily"—not just a sudden outburst that quickly passes, but constant dropping tears. Some translations have it "my soul slumbers." *Heaviness* (Strong's #H8424) means "grief, sadness, sorrow." This whole phrase aptly describes being worn down by the heaviness of life.

I'm pretty sure all of us at certain times have felt like we were being worn down by griefs and sorrows resulting from outward sources affecting our souls inwardly. Like a house under constant storms of steady falling rain eventually begins to leak. Again, can we all relate to this visual sometimes?

But again, the psalmist resorts to a reliance upon God's word to strengthen him. Without that infusion of the Almighty's endless strength, we are wholly left to natural remedy—we may patch the roof, as it were, but the rains keep coming. It's by appropriating God's boundless power that we stand firm under the storms of life.

✤ Day 127 ✤

"Finally, my brethren, be strong in the Lord and in the power of His might. Put on the whole armor of God, that you may be able to stand against the wiles of the devil."

Ephesians 6:10-11

Strong in the Lord" speaks of divine enablement, "receive strength from" the Lord Jesus Christ. Human strength is an exhaustible commodity. That doesn't mean human strength is "bad"—we should all do what we can in the natural, being wise to utilize our strength where it produces the most beneficial results: family, friends, work, our own selves, and so on.

However, we must realize that human strength is fleeting. Relying solely on our own abilities will eventually cause those abilities to run out of strength. If we find ourselves throwing strength at a situation that is not yielding a desired result, rather than continue flailing with our fists, we would do well to conserve our own strength and "be strong in the Lord," allowing Him to strengthen us out of His infinite reserves.

How do we "get" His strength? It comes out of intimacy with Him, spending time waiting (that is, serving) upon Him in worship. That may not seem like "activity," but when faced with life-storms, it is the most sensible action we can take. Save your strength and rely upon His.

❧ Day 128 ❧

"Finally, my brethren, be strong in the Lord and in the power of His might. Put on the whole armor of God, that you may be able to stand against the wiles of the devil."

Ephesians 6:10-11

*P*ower is "mighty deed, force, vigor, dominion." (Strong's #G2904) *Might* is akin to "the ability to hold in check," a derivative of a word meaning "to hold in the hand" or to possess force. (Strong's #G2479) Again, this power and might belong to Him, yielded "on loan" so to speak to His people so they may withstand the tricks of the enemy. *Wiles* is a compound word in the Greek: *meta* ("with, after, behind;" Strong's #G3326) and *hodeuo* ("journey, travel;" Strong's #G3593.) Where we get the English word *methods*. It means "lying in wait" or "traveling behind" and implies trickery, deceit, ambush. Spiritual armor is required to withstand these traps.

Power and might is conveyed by Paul's "whole armor" visual: truth, righteousness, peace, faith, salvation, the Word of God, prayer and supplication. (Verses 14-8) If we outline the keywords of this devotional, they are the "whole armor" of God, worn and applied correctly to the situation of need. The storms of life are often a method of the devil to trap you, but you have the power and might of godly armor to insulate you!

Day 129

"But those who wait on the LORD shall renew their strength; they shall mount up with wings like eagles, they shall run and not be weary, they shall walk and not faint."

Isaiah 40:31

*H*ere's that word "wait" again. Recall in the Hebrew it means "bind or twist together" (Strong's #H6960)—that is, those who "wrap themselves up in the LORD." The concept of multiplied strength is implied within the word in the sense of tying fast two things together to make them stronger. A double knot is stronger than a single one. Picture braiding strands of rope together to combine their individual level of strength. Layering two notes together to form a chord; the output sonically is doubly increased.

Wait conveys a sense of eager expectation, lingering in hope. Again, "waiting for Christmas morning" as opposed to "waiting in the dentist's office." These are the people who find renewed strength. *Renew* here is a great verb. Poetically, it means "to slip or glide through" (see Gesenius once again), implying slipperiness or smoothness due to fat—we might say "greasy" in today's parlance. It conveys the image of a blade of grass pushing through the soil, or a tree renewing its shiny leaves. Waiting on the LORD makes us spiritually greasy, able to slip through the storms of life. What a visual!

⇒⊷ Day 130 ⊶⇐

"But those who wait on the LORD shall renew their strength; they shall mount up with wings like eagles, they shall run and not be weary, they shall walk and not faint."

Isaiah 40:31

*W*ings like eagles" provides a fantastic visual here. I'm sure we've all seen, at least in photos or video, powerful birds of prey gliding upon the winds, scarcely flapping their wings as they soar high above the storms. They are hardly exerting strength while covering great distances. Eagles are considered apex predators, meaning they sit (glide?) at the top of the food chain. Because of the heights at which they soar, they are virtually unassailable by any predator in the animal kingdom.

The word "wings" (Strong's #H83) refers to the pinion feathers, as opposed to the appendage itself, and is translated "long-winged" in Ezekiel 17:3. It's compared to the similar word for "fly," which connotes passing over, high above, surpassing.

Whether running or walking, those who wait upon the Lord will not become wearied (which means "to gasp from labor") or tired ("fatigued, worn out.") It means to be kept in peak spiritual condition, gathering strength to spring high above the storms. What a great verse!

❧ Day 131 ❦

"God is our refuge and strength, a very present help in trouble. Therefore we will not fear, even though the earth be removed, and though the mountains be carried into the midst of the sea; though its waters roar and be troubled, though the mountains shake with its swelling. Selah."

Psalm 46:1-3

*R*efuge is from a root meaning "to flee for protection" (Strong's H2620), to hide out under the shadow of Someone greater for safety, to place yourself in the trust of Another. It's really the embodiment of the phrase "Shelter from the storm." It's the word "trust" in Psalm 73:28: "But it is good for me to draw near to God; I have put my trust in the LORD God, that I may declare all Your works." *Strength* speaks of the ability to prevail. (See Strong's #H5810.) *Very* is a masculine adjective meaning "exceeding force, muchness, to an abundant degree." (Strong's #H3966) *Present* most properly means "has come forth." (Strong's #H4672) It's not so much speaking of proximity as much as "He's proven Himself..." Help is the name Ezra: "to offer assistance." (Strong's #H5833) When we flee to God in the midst of storms we encounter His exceedingly forceful assistance to prevail.

✥ Day 132 ✥

"God is our refuge and strength, a very present help in trouble. Therefore we will not fear, even though the earth be removed, and though the mountains be carried into the midst of the sea; though its waters roar and be troubled, though the mountains shake with its swelling. Selah."

Psalm 46:1-3

If we take the phrase "very present help" to mean "He's been found to be an exceedingly forceful Help" in our troubles, we can compare that to the transience of those circumstances which cause us to fear. Even the earth, the mountains, the sea—those material creations which we view as effectively permanent, since they've been around far longer than we have and will remain long after we're gone—are in reality temporary and transitory compared to their Creator.

"For I am the LORD, I do not change…" (Malachi 3:6) "Heaven and earth will pass away, but My words will by no means pass away." (Matthew 24:35) This is called the immutability of God. This is the only bedrock we have to stand on that can never be eroded no matter what storms come against us. He has revealed Himself to be a "very present help in trouble," and that cannot be changed. You have nothing to fear so long as you've built your house upon the Rock. (See Matthew 7:24-27.)

❧ *Day 133* ❧

"Then he said to them, 'Go your way, eat the fat, drink the sweet, and send portions to those for whom nothing is prepared; for this day is holy to our Lord. Do not sorrow, for the joy of the LORD is your strength.'"

Nehemiah 8:10

The context of this passage recounts Ezra's reading of the Law in the hearing of all the Israelites. The Levites stood by his side to explain the meaning of the Law to the people. The passage shares that the people stood when the Book was opened, and it took from morning till noon to read through it and make sure the people understood what it was saying. Verse 9 says when the people heard the words of the Law, they wept. Their actions in honoring the Word, by standing, and their genuine emotional response to God's Word to them, by weeping, is worth noting. While historically the actions of the people of Israel are not ones we should always duplicate, in this instance their actions as one people *are* something we should endeavor to imitate. Many Christians who are sincere in their beliefs do not place an emphasis on the Word of God as they should. I know I've been guilty of this, and I don't think I'm the only one. A large portion of "shelter from the storms" stems directly from our discipline in honoring the Word. Make sure to spend time doing so!

☙ Day 134 ❧

"Then he said to them, 'Go your way, eat the fat, drink the sweet, and send portions to those for whom nothing is prepared; for this day is holy to our Lord. Do not sorrow, for the joy of the LORD is your strength.'"

Nehemiah 8:10

Nehemiah was governor (*Tirshatha*) of the people. After the Law had been read, they were all weeping, but he tells them not to be sorrowful, and rather, go to your homes and prepare a feast—not just a regular meal, but something fancy. And for those who have nothing, make sure to take care of them too.

When we give God's Word a place of preeminence in our lives, that obedience and honor to it creates a joy in our lives that carries over to others. Studying the Word is not out of a sense of legalism or obligation—it shows you that you are free in Christ, that your God cares deeply for you and watches over His Word to perform it in your life. That's to be celebrated! It's a privilege to live in the Word.

It is not the letter of the Law that is your strength—it is the joy of the Lord. Your shelter from the storms of life is not found in a system of religious rules and constrictions, but in a vibrant relationship with the Spirit as He unveils the truth of the Word to you.

❧ Day 135 ❧

"But You, O LORD, do not be far from Me; O My Strength, hasten to help Me! Deliver Me from the sword, My precious life from the power of the dog. Save Me from the lion's mouth and from the horns of the wild oxen! You have answered Me."

Psalm 22:19-21

King David, under the inspiration of the Holy Spirit, is prophesying the Messiah's words concerning His Passion. While remaining fully God, Jesus was also fully Man, reliant upon the Father for strength to hold up under the grueling and gruesome trials. His prayer should be ours—"Oh LORD, do not be far from us!" Our focus should be on our Strength more than our circumstances.

The word for *Strength* here is used only once in the OT. (Strong's #H360) It is a feminine form of the word translated *strength* in Psalm 88:4, also only used once. While both words do mean "strength," most properly the word in Psalm 22 signifies the power to protect.

When we are pressed and distressed by the storms of life, we need to turn our cries to God for protection, rather than rant at the situations: the swords, dogs, lions and oxen, as it were. Our energy is put to better use crying out, "O my Strength, hasten to help me!"

⊰ Day 136 ⊱

"But You, O Lᴏʀᴅ, do not be far from Me; O My Strength, hasten to help Me! Deliver Me from the sword, My precious life from the power of the dog. Save Me from the lion's mouth and from the horns of the wild oxen! You have answered Me."

Psalm 22:19-21

*M*y precious life" is translated *darling* in the KJV, meaning "my one and only." Our lives are singularly precious since they're the only ones we have. As God, Jesus understood the importance of His Passion; as a Man, He most certainly would've rather *not* faced them. While very few people today have undergone the kinds of trials Jesus faced, some of us are facing storms that could potentially be totally ruinous, even deadly. We need salvation and deliverance *now*. "Hasten to help Me!"

The way this Psalm closes out is a total shift from the way it starts. From "You have answered Me" onward we find the Shelter from the storm in action. That word *answered* properly means "to sing." (Strong's #H6030) It connotes to shout, announce, testify. When we cry out to God, we can expect more than just some trite, casual response. His power to protect is fully engaged in carrying us through the storm to the other side!

❧ *Day 137* ❧

*"Behold, God is my salvation, I will trust and not be afraid; for Y*AH*,
the L*ORD*, is my strength and song; He also has become my salvation."*

Isaiah 12:2

*T*his passage is repeated almost verbatim three times in
the OT: Exodus 15:2, Psalm 118:14 and here. These are
also the only times this word for *song* (Strong's #H2176) is
used. It refers not only to instrumental music, or a melody of
praise, but the Object of that praise. Because of His strength
given to us, we offer our praise unto Him. While we worship
God simply for being THE LORD, if He never did one thing for
us, thankfully He has become our salvation and deserves our
"song." Do not forget that a major component of finding shelter
from the storms is rooted in our praise and admiration for His
goodness, which includes the strength we are so desperately
seeking.

The repetition of *salvation* here places emphasis on what the
LORD has become for us: recall that the Hebrew word is where
we get the name Jesus, "He rescues." This is not accidental. It is
rescue in every sense of the word, in this life and the next. When
God came down as the Man Jesus Christ, He, in the most literal
sense, "became our salvation."

❧ Day 138 ❧

"Behold, God is my salvation, I will trust and not be afraid; for YAH, the LORD, is my strength and song; He also has become my salvation."

Isaiah 12:2

*B*eing afraid of the negative circumstances we face in life is the opposite of trusting in God. And while like many things in life, trusting in God is easier said than done, the truth is "he who fears has not been made perfect in love." (1 John 4:18) To "not be afraid" is a decision made in faith prior to not being afraid in actuality. The manifestation of fearlessness is a result of purposing in your heart to trust the Lord for your salvation, regardless of how you feel. So when you are confronted with a life storm, you *can* make the decision not to be fearful, and as you continue trusting in the Lord, you will begin to fear less. That trust and confidence in the face of adversity grows over time as you yield your fear to God. It is a work of the Holy Spirit as you continue to submit your emotions, including fear, to Him. It's interesting to note this is one of four times in the Bible the proper name of God is left untranslated as *Yah. Yah,* of course, is the abbreviation of *Yahweh.* Like "salvation," the repetition of His Name, *Yah Yehovah,* places emphasis on the reality that He is the unchanging Origin of salvation and the truth that we can be unafraid.

❧ Day 139 ❦

"O Lord, be gracious to us; we have waited for You. Be their arm every morning, our salvation also in the time of trouble."

Isaiah 33:2

G racious (Strong's #H2603) can be compared to a similar word in the Hebrew meaning "to bend down" or decline; it's used for *encamp* or *pitch a tent* in the Bible. It gives the thought image of God abiding among us and showing mercy or pity to us in our situations. Again, *waited* implies knitting ourselves together with God, cohabitating with Him, in expectancy of that merciful favor, to tarry with Him until that grace is manifested. It is an active verb, signifying *gathering* together with the Lord, *collecting* grace from Him. (Strong's #H6960)

The relationship between Jesus and His followers is frequently described as a marriage in the Bible. Earthly marriages are a joining together for strength, support, and communion. The relationship we have with God is similar, except in our union with Him, we reap the benefit of His beneficence; and while we don't give Him strength or support, we *do* provide the communion He is longing for with His creation. That communion unlocks the magnanimity we need from Him.

❧ Day 140 ❧

"O LORD, be gracious to us; we have waited for You. Be their arm every morning, our salvation also in the time of trouble."

Isaiah 33:2

*T*he marginalia shows *their* as *our*—the pronoun is omitted in some manuscripts, but the context makes it clear this is a prayer for "us" today, intended as a prophetic declaration from the past for future peoples of God; that is, *us.*

While we are entwining ourselves with the LORD, we are asking that He would be our arm every morning. *Arm* in the Hebrew is specifically speaking of an outstretched forearm, signifying strength or power. (Strong's #H2220) The idea conveyed here is our contrary circumstances being "strong-armed" out of the way by God. This is to be our prayer *every morning,* the first thought as daylight dawns and we arise: Lord, be my arm today!

Further, in a specific "time of trouble," we pray for His salvation. That phrase speaks of individual occurrences, or seasons, of adversity, and sometimes it's translated *evening*— seasons of darker times, see? So the LORD's grace, His arm, His salvation, is for us all day, every day, morning to night, and it is renewed every morning for the next day. (Lamentations 3:22-23)

❧ Day 141 ❧

"Though the fig tree may not blossom, nor fruit be on the vines; though the labor of the olive may fail, and the fields yield no food; though the flock may be cut off from the fold, and there be no herd in the stalls—yet I will rejoice in the LORD, I will joy in the God of my salvation. The LORD God is my strength; He will make my feet like deer's feet, and He will make me walk on my high hills…"

Habakkuk 3:17-19

The phrase "under his vine and under his fig tree" (see 1 Kings 4:25) means to dwell in safety and tranquility, so all these "bad things" listed in the passage are poetic descriptions from an agrarian society on the loss of not only physical sustenance, but also security and welfare. Most of us, in Western society especially, are not physically starving, but the application of these verses when faced with life-storms is appropriate. *Blossom* speaks of flourishing, growing. *Fruit* speaks of increase and wealth. These descriptions convey the fruits of our labor being denied to us. We can sum all this up to say: the storms of life, right?

Habakkuk is reminding himself (and us) that in real, or metaphorical, famine, we find salvation and deliverance in the Lord. No matter what you are facing today, He will not leave you in a state of dearth as long as you stay connected to Him!

❧ Day 142 ❧

"Though the fig tree may not blossom, nor fruit be on the vines; though the labor of the olive may fail, and the fields yield no food; though the flock may be cut off from the fold, and there be no herd in the stalls—yet I will rejoice in the LORD, I will joy in the God of my salvation. The LORD God is my strength; He will make my feet like deer's feet, and He will make me walk on my high hills…"

Habakkuk 3:17-19

*H*abakkuk's statement of faith is a commitment to be joyful, finding strength and stability in God's promise of salvation from the storms he faced. Based on His trustworthiness, we can also make a commitment to be joyful in the face of adversity. *Rejoice* is "exultation in triumphing" (Strong's #H5937) in the face of difficulties. The emphasis in this word is on the sound of rejoicing, exclaiming buoyantly that you will be victorious. Knowing that you are going to prevail against any onslaught you face creates a joyful exuberance *during* the storm. You should shout your victory in the face of your trials—your God is your strength and salvation! *Joy* most properly means "to spin round in a circle from emotion." (Strong's #H1523) Rejoicing and joying yield God's strength, lifting you above the storms to walk as surefooted as the deer on a lofty hill of safety and tranquility. Rejoice and joy in the LORD!

❧ Day 143 ❧

"...That He would grant you, according to the riches of His glory, to be strengthened with might through His Spirit in the inner man, that Christ may dwell in your hearts through faith; that you, being rooted and grounded in love...may be filled with all the fullness of God."

Ephesians 3:16-17,19

This passage shows the Trinity in action on your behalf. Colossians 2:9-10 states, "For in Him [Jesus] dwells all the fullness of the Godhead bodily; and you are complete in Him, who is the head of all principality and power." [brackets author's own] This prayer in Ephesians is that we may be "filled with Christ." The ability to be filled with Christ is granted by the Father, according to His glory (or because of "His great worth")—it's because of His great worth that He provided the means we might be filled with Christ. This ability to receive the fullness of Christ is imparted by the Holy Spirit into your spirit-man when you put your faith in Him. The outward expression of that infilling is strength and might, which are rooted and grounded in faith and love, in every facet of day-to-day life. When we are pressed by contrary circumstances, the strength and might, faith and love, to overcome them is found in the full manifestation of the Godhead represented in Christ.

⚛ *Day 144* ⚛

"...That He would grant you, according to the riches of His glory, to be strengthened with might through His Spirit in the inner man, that Christ may dwell in your hearts through faith; that you, being rooted and grounded in love...may be filled with all the fullness of God."

Ephesians 3:16-17,19

This passage also shows the trinity of our experience in God: starting with the *inner man* (Strong's #G2080), which is the conscience of the soul, your spirit coming into contact with His Spirit. This is how you relate to God. The *heart* (Strong's #G2588) is your faculty of understanding, your thoughts and motivations, the soul as it connects to you coming into contact with Christ by faith. This is how you relate to yourself. These two connections (of the spirit and of the soul—the mind, will, and emotions) are rooted in love, which goes beyond your *knowledge* (Strong's #G1108); that is, your soul as it connects to the world around you. This is how you relate to others. This "outward man" is influenced by the inner man and the heart and equally affects your interactions in the natural world. Thus, "shelter from the storm" begins internally, filters through your five senses, and is expressed in your reactions to those you come in contact with.

❧ *Day 145* ❧

"Strengthen the weak hands, and make firm the feeble knees. Say to those who are fearful-hearted, 'Be strong, do not fear! Behold, your God will come with vengeance, with the recompense of God; He will come and save you.'"

Isaiah 35:3-4

*I*n this passage, God promises direct intervention in our lives. Twice it is mentioned "He will come," which is used for strong emphasis: God **WILL** come, God **WILL** come. It's like when Jesus says, "Verily, verily" or "Truly, truly" in the Gospels. The repetition denotes, "This is real and important, pay attention here!" Salvation, in all its facets pertaining to daily life on this earthly realm (and the afterlife in the spiritual realm), is guaranteed for those who trust in the Lord—He has to be "your God" individually for this promise to be in effect. It's not automatic for everyone.

But it's important to note that it's *God Himself* who is coming. It shows that the Almighty is concerned about your life affairs and is directly influencing your negative circumstances by obtaining vengeance and giving recompence. The word *come* in the Hebrew (Strong's #H935) carries a militant connotation: "to fall upon and attack an enemy" or "to go down to war." This passage promises God will be your mighty Warrior in time of need.

❧ Day 146 ❧

"Strengthen the weak hands, and make firm the feeble knees. Say to those who are fearful-hearted, 'Be strong, do not fear! Behold, your God will come with vengeance, with the recompense of God; He will come and save you.'"

Isaiah 35:3-4

*U*nquestionably, this passage is messianic prophecy, speaking of the Incarnation of God in Jesus Christ. But it's also a continuous promise through the ages that Christ provides recompense (or "repayment, restitution, reimbursement, reward") for what the enemy has stolen from His people. Vengeance is the LORD's. (Deuteronomy 32:35)

Therefore, our focus is not to be in "smiting our enemies"—leave that to Him—but to strengthen our weak hands and make firm our feeble knees. *Weak* means "sinking or dropping" hands. (Strong's #H7503) *Feeble* is "stumbling, tottering" knees. (Strong's #H3782) *Fearful-hearted* means "hasty hearted" (Strong's #H4116) and implies fleeing before an enemy—that is, to run away from a problem instead of standing firm during a stormy crisis. Our job is to "be strong, do no fear" in the midst of adverse circumstances, being firmly persuaded that God will come; yes, God will come! And we will be rescued and repaid for our troubles.

❧ *Day 147* ❧

*"The stone which the builders rejected has become the chief cornerstone. This was the L*ORD*'s doing; it is marvelous in our eyes. This is the day the L*ORD *has made; we will rejoice and be glad in it. Save now, I pray, O L*ORD*; O L*ORD*, I pray, send now prosperity. Blessed is he who comes in the name of the L*ORD*!"*

Psalm 118:24

*A*nother messianic prophecy that finds fulfillment in Jesus Christ, the chief Cornerstone. Again, "This was the LORD's doing" shows that salvation, represented in Christ, stems from *His* glory, His purpose and plan put into motion. All we can do is marvel at it. The phrase means "This is from the LORD." In His complete understanding of all times and all places simultaneously, God *knew* what He was doing in providing the rescue Jesus offers to all people, everywhere and every moment. When we can comprehend even the most infinitesimal part of God's omniscience, omnipresence and omnipotence (that's a lot of omnis), it yields a sense of security and peace because we know no storms we face will ever catch Him off guard or unprepared to offer us the salvation we need. It appears to us that God has created a special event that produces our deliverance from the storm, but in reality, He had already secured it from the foundation of the world. (See Revelation 13:8.)

❧ Day 148 ❧

"The stone which the builders rejected has become the chief cornerstone. This was the LORD's doing; it is marvelous in our eyes. This is the day the LORD has made; we will rejoice and be glad in it. Save now, I pray, O LORD; O LORD, I pray, send now prosperity. Blessed is he who comes in the name of the LORD!"

Psalm 118:24

*M*arvelous most properly means "separated, distinguished" (Strong's #H6381) and conveys completing a hard or difficult task. It's the same word translated "Is anything too hard for the LORD?" in Genesis 18:14. The same power that permitted Abraham and Sarah to conceive in old age is the same power brought to bear in this "day the Lord has made" for your salvation and prosperity. This *day* (Strong's #H3117) is especially created for us at *this* time, right now. While the word in the Hebrew can literally mean "day"— the time when the sun is up—it's also figuratively used for a special "season" as in an "accepted time," a "day of salvation." (See 2 Corinthians 6:2.)

God has provided the means for your deliverance through the storms of life by the power of the chief Cornerstone. You are living in the day of salvation. *Now* is that time, *now* is that day. He's made it specifically for you. Rejoice and be glad in it!

❧ *Day 149* ❧

"For I know the thoughts that I think toward you, says the LORD, thoughts of peace and not of evil, to give you a future and a hope. Then you will call upon Me and go and pray to Me, and I will listen to you. And you will seek Me and find Me, when you search for Me with all your heart."

Jeremiah 29:11-13

Says the LORD" is a strong phrase. It asserts these words came directly to Jeremiah from God Himself, beyond just the prophet's own thoughts, making them an unassailable decree. God puts His Word above His name (Psalm 138:2), so when He ties Himself to a promise, it cannot be broken, so long as the conditions of that promise are met. When an OT prophet used "says the LORD," they were putting their own life on the line. (Deuteronomy 18:20) Therefore, we can take this passage as 100% truth, direct communication from God, which means we ought to pay attention, right?

Taking this passage as God's own words, we then find that He is thinking about His people. That, in and of itself, is comforting—we're not forgotten by God or dismissed out of His mind. Further, His thoughts toward us are not "evil thoughts;" rather, His thoughts are peaceable. We must know—really *know*—that God wants our peace and will work to that end.

⇾ *Day 150* ⇽

"For I know the thoughts that I think toward you, says the LORD, *thoughts of peace and not of evil, to give you a future and a hope. Then you will call upon Me and go and pray to Me, and I will listen to you. And you will seek Me and find Me, when you search for Me with all your heart."*

Jeremiah 29:11-13

uture and hope" in the KJV is translated "expected end." Though it's an accurate translation, the NKJV is perhaps a better rendering, as the word for *expected* is what we've studied more than once in this devotional: *hope* as a "cord" that binds us to the Lord. *End* is used prophetically for a "future time," an "event for posterity." (Strong's #H319) In the most modern parlance, we could say God's thoughts are to provide a peaceful, hopeful future for His people. (See Jeremiah 31:17.)

That sounds wonderful! What are the conditions, then, to entering into this hopeful future of peace? Calling upon the LORD in prayer, we are assured He *will* listen. If we seek Him, we *will* find Him. If we search for Him with all our heart, He *will* be found. (See Jeremiah 29:14.) Shelter from the storm is available to us when we wholeheartedly seek Him.

Day 151

"Oh, taste and see that the LORD is good; blessed is the man who trusts in Him! Oh, fear the LORD, you His saints! There is no want to those who fear Him. The young lions lack and suffer hunger; but those who seek the LORD shall not lack any good thing."

Psalm 34:8-10

"Taste and see" is not just a poetic phrase. It means to "perceive by the senses of taste and sight." (Strong's #H2938) It's to be an actual occurrence, not an idea we have. We know cookies from the oven are good, not because someone's told us, but because we can see, smell, taste them for ourselves. It signifies more than just a casual, passing glance, some tiny nibble, of the Lord's goodness; but rather, to experience Him firsthand through the tangible senses. We're to *relish* His kindness and mercy concretely in our daily lives—not just give mental assent to an abstract concept: "Yeah, God is good. I'll see it when I get to heaven." That expectation provides no shelter from the storms of this life.

Jesus admonished His followers, "Most assuredly, I say to you, unless you eat the flesh of the Son of Man and drink His blood, you have no life in you." (John 6:53) It's been taught by worthy theologians that means to *devour* the Lord's goodness like a starving person. Taste and see!

☙ Day 152 ❧

"Oh, taste and see that the LORD is good; blessed is the man who trusts in Him! Oh, fear the LORD, you His saints! There is no want to those who fear Him. The young lions lack and suffer hunger; but those who seek the LORD shall not lack any good thing."

Psalm 34:8-10

*D*efining *good* as it pertains to God in this passage speaks of being "agreeable to the senses," "pleasant to the higher nature," to have "understanding intellectually" of His goodness. (Strong's #H2896) It goes beyond just physical sustenance—although that's definitely included in the definition in these verses—but we're told that if we seek Him, we shall not lack *any* good thing. God's provisions for us satisfy our bodies, minds, souls and spirits—across the board, in all facets of life. Shelter, indeed! So how do we "taste and see" all this goodness?

First, *fearing* Him, in proper reverence and honor. We stated earlier, it's more than just fearing God will punish you. It's *wanting* to do what is pleasing in His sight. (1 John 3:22) This is the starting place of wisdom. (Proverbs 9:10) Second, *seeking* Him. This means to "tread frequently" with Him (Strong's #H1875), to study with practical application, diligently inquire. Those who do these things will lack nothing. What a reward!

❧ *Day 153* ❧

"For our light affliction, which is but for a moment, is working for us a far more exceeding and eternal weight of glory, while we do not look at the things which are seen, but at the things which are not seen. For the things which are seen are temporary, but the things which are not seen are eternal."

2 Corinthians 4:17-18

L ight affliction" is not patronizing concerning the difficulties we go through. They are real adversities. But Paul, who outlines some of his afflictions in 2 Corinthians 11, focuses on the transitory nature of those troubles. The word *light* (Strong's #G1645) appears to be a derivative of words meaning "to carry" and "less;" that is, "easier to bear." The difficulties we face, which are subject to change, are easier to bear in light of the eternal glory that is pouring through us as "earthen vessels." (Verse 7)

To be channels for the glory of God to pour through should be the prime objective of the Christian's lifestyle. *Glory* (Strong's #G1391) speaks of an opinion of someone's worth, in this case, God's. We have the distinct privilege of being conduits for God's "kingly majesty" to be revealed to the world at large, so that they have a good opinion of His worth. Such an honor makes the passing storms of life easier to bear.

Day 154

"For our light affliction, which is but for a moment, is working for us a far more exceeding and eternal weight of glory, while we do not look at the things which are seen, but at the things which are not seen. For the things which are seen are temporary, but the things which are not seen are eternal."

2 Corinthians 4:17-18

*E*xceeding and eternal" is superlative in the Greek. Paul uses extreme words to intensely emphasize the "weight" and "glory" that God causes to rest upon us. In the Hebrew, *weight* and *glory* are the same word, signifying the heaviness of God's eternal worth and magnificence, His power and authority, bearing down on His people. How humbling that God chooses to use us as outlets for that glory! But notice how that glory comes: from the light afflictions—they "work" for us (that is, "bring about," Strong's #G2716) this extreme weightiness of God's reputation manifesting through us. No one likes the storms we face, but the effect they produce in us is worth the temporary discomfort. Paul juxtaposes the "temporary" storms with the "eternal" glory and declares the former is not worth "looking at" when compared with the latter. We, too, should keep this view when the challenges arise.

❧ Day 155 ❧

"What then shall we say to these things? If God is for us, who can be against us? He who did not spare His own Son, but delivered Him up for us all, how shall He not with Him also freely give us all things?"

Romans 8:31-32

Concluding his discourse on suffering versus revealed glory (Verses 18-25) and delineating the help of the Holy Spirit in our weaknesses (Verses 26-27), Paul summarizes ("What shall we say...") these two concepts by proposing two rhetorical questions. The answers are "no one" and "He will."

If the primary purpose of life-storms is to draw us closer to Jesus so that more of His glory can flow through us, we see that even in hardships, God is "for us." That's where we get the word *hyper* (Strong's #G5228), which means "over and above, very exceedingly, chiefest." There is no partway with God. You're either born again, or you're not. So when God puts His glory in the midst of our infirmities, He's *all in.*

Everything that He is, which is *hyper,* is brought to bear against your enemy. In light of that truth, no weapon formed against you shall prosper. (Isaiah 54:17) There is no downside to going *all in* with God.

❧ *Day 156* ❦

"What then shall we say to these things? If God is for us, who can be against us? He who did not spare His own Son, but delivered Him up for us all, how shall He not with Him also freely give us all things?"

Romans 8:31-32

What proof does Paul give to assure his readers that God is all "for us"? The fact that God the Father did not spare His own Son from trial, even to the point of crucifixion, but raised Him up (Acts 2:24) and gave Him the place of preeminence above all things. (Ephesians 1:20) The Father loves the Son (John 3:35; 5:20) so it must have been difficult to deliver Him up to the most extreme storms of life anyone's ever faced. Why did He do this? "For us all."

Since there's no halfway with God, Jesus threw Himself into our circumstances *completely*, even offering His own body to be tortured, submitting to the pain and humiliation of crucifixion, knowing that His Father would "do right" by Him and raise Him up, thereby securing the means to "freely give us all things." All means "all." If you accept that He's done this for you, then you should also accept that if He's for you, nothing can stand against you. You *will* triumph over any adversity because you're in Christ. (2 Corinthians 2:14) You cannot be defeated!

ᵔᴥᵔ *Day 157* ᵔᴥᵔ

"Yet in all these things we are more than conquerors through Him who loved us. For I am persuaded that neither death nor life, nor angels nor principalities nor powers, nor things present nor things to come, nor height nor depth, nor any other created thing, shall be able to separate us from the love of God which is in Christ Jesus our Lord."

Romans 8:37-39

"All these things" are "...tribulation, or distress, or persecution, or famine, or nakedness, or peril, or sword" (Verse 35), which sum up the storms of life. We are "more than conquerors"—that word *hyper* again—over "all these things" through Christ because of His love for us. All of God's glory and power, holiness and righteousness, is rooted in His love.

You probably know the Greek word is *agapao*. (Strong's #G25) It appears to be derived from *phileo*, which you'll recognize as "brotherly love" and the prefix *agan*, which means "much"—so it's referring to a higher order of love in a moral, right sense as opposed to sentiment or feeling. It's this type of love that *remains*. (1 Corinthians 13:13) *Agapao* means "to welcome, entertain, be fond of, love dearly." Because of this love, God makes His children "more than conquerors" of "all these things."

❧ Day 158 ❧

"Yet in all these things we are more than conquerors through Him who loved us. For I am persuaded that neither death nor life, nor angels nor principalities nor powers, nor things present nor things to come, nor height nor depth, nor any other created thing, shall be able to separate us from the love of God which is in Christ Jesus our Lord."

Romans 8:37-39

Nothing, absolutely nothing, can separate us from the love God has for us in Christ. *Separate* (Strong's #G5563) comes from the word for "chasm, gulf," speaking of the empty space between two points of land. It's used for divorce between a married couple: "to depart, go away." Paul's poetic list of what cannot separate us from God's love in Christ is exhaustive, covering every storm we could face—death, life, spirits, past things, present things, future things, physical distance, *any* created thing—none of this divorces you from God's love through Jesus.

I can think of no more comforting fact than this. I am as "persuaded" as Paul, we will conquer any and every adversary set against us because of God's indissoluble love for us, represented in sum total through the Lord Jesus Christ. You gain every advantage under creation in accepting this truth. Be persuaded!

❧ Day 159 ❦

"Through the LORD's *mercies we are not consumed, because His compassions fail not. They are new every morning; great is Your faithfulness. 'The* LORD *is my portion,' says my soul, 'therefore I hope in Him!'"*

Lamentations 3:22-24

*C*ontextually, this chapter at first glance seems pretty bleak and dark. It's definitely a lamentation. The poetic descriptions of the prophet's miseries under the wrath of God seem like life-storms amplified to hurricane proportions! However, the part that provides shelter from the storms is when he recalls to mind (Verse 21) that he is not consumed by these troubles, and it gives him hope.

Consumed, in both a good (as in "consumed with zeal") and bad sense ("to be destroyed"), means "to be completed, to finish wholly." (Strong's #H8552) We all have situations and circumstances we would rather not face, but if we "recall to mind" the faithfulness of the Lord, we are able to take heart in the truth that His mercies are renewed every morning and we are to wait in hope for the salvation of the Lord (Verse 26), because He is trustworthy to bring it to pass. We will not be consumed because His mercy and compassion do not fail: they also cannot be wholly consumed, praise God!

❧ Day 160 ❧

"Through the LORD's mercies we are not consumed, because His compassions fail not. They are new every morning; great is Your faithfulness. 'The LORD is my portion,' says my soul, 'therefore I hope in Him!'"

Lamentations 3:22-24

*J*esus admonishes His followers, "Therefore do not worry about tomorrow, for tomorrow will worry about its own things. Sufficient for the day is its own trouble." (Matthew 6:34) Since the LORD's compassion and mercy are new every morning, that shows us His grace as a shelter from the storm is day-by-day. This isn't a mark of stinginess, certainly not! Rather, it shows His commitment to us each day—it will not fail, ever. Therefore, our relationship to God is also renewed on a daily basis, a reaffirmation that we belong to Him, and Him alone, every time we wake up.

The word *portion* (Strong's #H2506) comes from a root meaning "to be smooth" and defined the smooth stones used to cast lots to distribute, or divide up, something. It means an "allotment, award, possession, inheritance." Again, this shows a daily portioning out of God's mercy and compassion to each of His people. We have hope in that expectancy. (See Psalm 145:15-16.)

"Therefore we do not lose heart. Even though our outward man is perishing, yet the inward man is being renewed day by day."

2 Corinthians 4:16

*L*ose heart" is probably better rendered in the KJV, "faint not," even though the Greek does signify "losing heart." The word (Strong's #G1573) is a compound of a preposition meaning "out of, from" and a word meaning "intrinsically worthless." Most succinctly the word implies "completely bad" and implies one becoming totally weak, faint of heart, wholly wearied or exhausted. The adverse conditions we face in life can have the effect of wearing us out to the point where we're utterly ineffective—this is the enemy's plan for you. (See Daniel 7:25) To pummel you with life-storms till you're put out of commission.

But the "therefore" shows *why* we do not "lose heart." The context of Paul's discourse is that we have the same "[S]pirit of faith" who "raised up the Lord Jesus" and who will also raise us up. (Verses 13-14) (See Romans 8:11.) Intimacy with the Holy Spirit in prayer, specifically in a heavenly prayer language, keeps us from fainting when besieged by the enemy's storms. This will ensure we are "renewed day by day."

❧ Day 162 ❧

"Therefore we do not lose heart. Even though our outward man is perishing, yet the inward man is being renewed day by day."

2 Corinthians 4:16

*P*erishing quite literally means "to rot," and by implication here means "changing for the worse." (Strong's #G1311) The "outward man" speaks of the body, the shell that contains the "inward man"—that is, the spirit. Your true self, your spirit, is imperishable and cannot rot when you place your faith in the life-giving Spirit of Jesus Christ. (1 Corinthians 15:45) The body, however, is liable to corruption, and the agents of this "perishing" in the context of this passage are the storms of life (see Verses 8-9); however, Paul is showing a conversion of life here: though the outward man is assailed, the inward man converts that "perishing" into renewal day by day.

How we convert the perishing into renewal is by obedience to God's decree that we share the light of the gospel with everyone we come in contact with. (Mark 16:15) It's not just witnessing or evangelizing, as vital as that is, but by witnessing *with our lifestyle* to those we spend our day-to-day lives with. As we do so, the "perishing" externally is converted into renewal inwardly each and every day.

❧ *Day 163* ❧

"Watch, stand fast in the faith, be brave, be strong. Let all that you do be done with love."

1 Corinthians 16:13-14

*W*atch in the Greek is where we get the name Gregory. (Strong's #G1127) The stem of the word means "rise up, awaken, rouse," and it speaks of gathering one's faculties, being vigilant, wakeful. Paul's exhortation is something frequently overlooked in the Christian's life—being constantly observant, wary for any life-storm that may suddenly develop around us. By being attentive to our surroundings, many flareups (not all) can be headed off before they erupt into full-blown squalls.

Oftentimes adverse situations arise not from poor decisions or bad actions, or even from circumstances beyond our control, but from simply being less observant of our relationships or the surrounding environments. We miss the signals that a storm is brewing until it's too late. The enemy will use any means at its disposal to get an inroad into causing trouble, not just reckless sin or stirring up unbelief, but even something as seemingly innocuous as not paying attention. This is why the Bible admonishes us to always be on guard and give no place whatsoever to the enemy. (See Ephesians 4:27.)

※ *Day 164* ※

"Watch, stand fast in the faith, be brave, be strong. Let all that you do be done with love."

1 Corinthians 16:13-14

Stand fast comes from the perfect tense of a word meaning "to be stationary." (Strong's #G4739) To be unwaveringly persistent in one's faith. While Jesus is the Author and Perfecter of our faith (Hebrews 12:2), there is a decision made on our part not to waver in our belief that God is the Shelter from our storms.

It is from the stance of watchfulness and resoluteness that the rest of this command springs: "be brave, be strong." Bravery in the face of danger often stems from preparedness. The more one is on watch, the less one is caught off guard, and fearfulness is diminished because we are ready to spring into action at the first whiff of a storm in the air. Strength as the Lord has it comes to us specifically through faith in His trustworthiness. His strength imbuing ours is proportionate to our faith in His character as revealed by the Word.

Lastly, all of our actions—watching, standing, being brave, being strong—are to be rooted in love. Being watchful and firm shouldn't come from an attitude of fault-finding or mistrust. Love conquers all. (See 1 Corinthians 13.)

✣ *Day 165* ✣

"Now to Him who is able to do exceedingly abundantly above all that we ask or think, according to the power that works in us, to Him be glory in the church by Christ Jesus to all generations, forever and ever. Amen."

Ephesians 3:20-21

I can ask and think pretty big, how about you? There are areas of our lives that we are all seeking enlargement. The desire to want growth, magnification, amplitude is not necessarily an improper motivation. Nearly all of us could use a little more money, a better job, improvement in our familial relationships and friendships, stronger immune systems, more sleep, the list goes on and on. Without striving for improvement in all these areas, we become stagnant and eventually begin to lose even what we have.

That is the context of Matthew 13:12, the hidden truths of the kingdom of Heaven, which include all these things mentioned above and so much more. This is why Jesus tells us to seek first the kingdom of God and His righteousness, then all these other things will be added as well. (See Matthew 6:33.) We know the kingdom of God is more than eating and drinking (Romans 14:17) but thank God He isn't stingy with *any* of His blessings. You are free to ask and think big!

❧ *Day 166* ❦

"Now to Him who is able to do exceedingly abundantly above all that we ask or think, according to the power that works in us, to Him be glory in the church by Christ Jesus to all generations, forever and ever. Amen."

Ephesians 3:20-21

*E*xceedingly abundantly" sounds wonderful! The Greek uses four adjectives (something like "*hyper, very highly, extraordinarily, exceedingly hyper*") to convey the superlative, consummate, unrivalled power that works *in us* through Christ Jesus. It is both mind-blowing and humbling to grasp even the smallest measure of the authority Jesus has granted to us through His name.

He grants to us this exceeding, abundant power for *His* own glory, because it brings honor and fame to His name when His followers have surplus power to share with "all generations, forever and ever." While I am not ultra-prosperity in my theology, in a "name it, claim it" sense, it certainly does not negate the truth that God is able to do hyper, hyper above what we can ask or think to bring Him glory. When you accept the responsibility of presenting that delegated authority to the world around you, no storm you face can seem overwhelming when compared to His glory and power flowing through your life, so ask and think big!

❧ Day 167 ❧

"But what things were gain to me, these I have counted loss for Christ. Yet indeed I also count all things loss for the excellence of the knowledge of Christ Jesus my Lord, for whom I have suffered the loss of all things, and count them as rubbish, that I may gain Christ…"

Philippians 3:7-8

*B*efore his Damascus Road experience, Paul had an awful lot going for him: well-born from good stock, a real "Jew's Jew," well-educated, well-respected among his peers, full of righteous zeal in persecuting those weird, cultish Christians, blameless according to the Law. He was doing all right for himself before Jesus zapped him and told him, "It's hard for you to kick against the goads" (Acts 26:14), which as a modern proverb would go, "You're sure a stubborn ox, aren't you?"

From that moment on, everything he'd ever been, ever had, ever enjoyed, became worthless to him—it was all "rubbish." The literal rendering is "like dog excrement." (Strong's #G4657) (Paul wasn't always urbane in his writings.) The point here, as it pertains to life-storms, is that nothing you are, nothing you have, in and of yourself, can provide lasting shelter—only "gaining Christ." If you count everything else as "loss," you gain so much more in Him!

❦ Day 168 ❧

"But what things were gain to me, these I have counted loss for Christ. Yet indeed I also count all things loss for the excellence of the knowledge of Christ Jesus my Lord, for whom I have suffered the loss of all things, and count them as rubbish, that I may gain Christ..."

Philippians 3:7-8

*K*nowledge in the Greek (Strong's #G1108) is more than just knowing the facts about something. It speaks of true understanding, perceiving; the root word speaks of feeling, as in experiential knowledge. It's to know that you know something. The act of knowing itself. It's one thing to know the thermometer tells you it's hot outside. It's quite another thing to know it because you're outside sweating in the heat. Both are important, but one is knowledge you've put into action through experience.

Many Christians, while they may *know* that Christ is their All-in-All, as in a general kind of knowledge or mental assent, do not *know* this by experience. Their perception, or understanding, of Christ Jesus as Lord is not as tangible as it needs to be to really declare He is their Shelter from the storm. We must experience the "excellence of the knowledge" in order to declare everything else is "rubbish" compared to that. Do not let fear, disbelief, or sin keep you from gaining Christ in a real, powerful way.

☙ *Day 169* ❧

"Beloved, if our heart does not condemn us, we have confidence toward God. And whatever we ask we receive from Him, because we keep His commandments and do those things that are pleasing in His sight. And this is His commandment: that we should believe on the name of His Son Jesus Christ and love one another, as He gave us commandment."

1 John 3:21-23

*C*ondemnation is the destroyer of confidence. *Condemn* is a compound word in the Greek meaning having "knowledge against" someone. (Strong's #G2607) It's the same kind of knowledge outlined in the previous day's entry, but here it carries the significance of faultfinding, having reason to lay blame on someone. When we find fault with ourselves, we lose that confidence we have toward God. Condemnation does no good for anyone other than to pass a sentence of limitation upon themselves. There *are* valid reasons we all have for condemning ourselves, but the wonderfulness of God's salvation through Jesus Christ renders that verdict of "condemned" null and void. If He forgives our trespasses, then we must also forgive our trespasses. When we do, that confidence to ask and expect to receive is restored. Don't condemn yourself for your past—He doesn't. (See John 8:11.)

Day 170

"Beloved, if our heart does not condemn us, we have confidence toward God. And whatever we ask we receive from Him, because we keep His commandments and do those things that are pleasing in His sight. And this is His commandment: that we should believe on the name of His Son Jesus Christ and love one another, as He gave us commandment."

1 John 3:21-23

Freedom from condemnation does not give license to continue giving cause for condemnation. That would be foolish in the extreme. Note, again, John 8:11: "Neither do I condemn you; go and sin no more." "Whatever we ask we receive from Him" is contingent upon "because we keep His commandments and do the things that are pleasing in His sight." Only from there can we have confidence to ask and receive.

Further, if He forgives our trespasses, we in turn must forgive the trespasses of others (Matthew 6:14-15)—that's why "love one another" is a commandment equal to faith in Jesus Christ. (Mark 12:29-31) "If I do this for you, you have to do it for others." God is vehemently opposed to condemnation in all its facets. Why? Because He knows it blocks receiving from Him. Shelter from the storms is directly proportionate to your faith, obedience, confidence and love. Guard them zealously!

☙ *Day 171* ❧

"Behold what manner of love the Father has bestowed on us, that we should be called children of God! Therefore the world does not know us, because it did not know Him. Beloved, now we are children of God; and it has not yet been revealed what we shall be, but we know that when He is revealed, we shall be like Him, for we shall see Him as He is. And everyone who has this hope in Him purifies himself, just as He is pure."

1 John 3:1-3

How do you know you've encountered Almighty God? You want to be like Him; it's a natural response to a supernatural experience—"I believe there is a God in heaven, now what does He want from me?" To believe in God and yet not bother to find out what He thinks about your relationship with Him is ludicrous. The "world does not know" part is speaking of people who have chosen to disregard Him, either by disbelief or willful rebellion. All people are either one or the other: the children of God or the children of the devil. (Verse 10) There is no partway with God.

Again, loving God completely and loving your fellow man is the litmus test of being called "children of God." For the children of God, the Gift of Jesus Christ is given, and thus the Promise of shelter from the storm. Do not forget, you are a child of God, reared in love!

✤ *Day 172* ✤

"Behold what manner of love the Father has bestowed on us, that we should be called children of God! Therefore the world does not know us, because it did not know Him. Beloved, now we are children of God; and it has not yet been revealed what we shall be, but we know that when He is revealed, we shall be like Him, for we shall see Him as He is. And everyone who has this hope in Him purifies himself, just as He is pure."

1 John 3:1-3

For the child of God, the singular aim in life is to "put on Christ" (Galatians 3:26-27; Colossians 3:12-14; Romans 13:14) and purify oneself as "He is pure." We want to be like Him, completely connected to the Father in love, and therefore receiving the power of the Father in every circumstance in life. And of course, the ultimate consummation of this truth is when "He is revealed" and we shall be "like Him" at the end of this age, whenever that should be.

However, *now* "we are the children of God." That means all of the benefits our loving Parent can bestow belong to us *now*. Again, there is no partway with God. You have every benefit of Jesus' salvation for your daily life in the present. His already sufficient shelter can only grow larger from this moment forward as you continue "putting Him on" until you meet Him face-to-face.

Day 173

"Therefore, brethren, having boldness to enter the Holiest by the blood of Jesus, by a new and living way which He consecrated for us, through the veil, that is, His flesh, and having a High Priest over the house of God, let us draw near with a true heart in full assurance of faith, having our hearts sprinkled from an evil conscience and our bodies washed with pure water. Let us hold fast the confession of our hope without wavering, for He who promised is faithful."

Hebrews 10:19-23

Boldness is one of the greatest benefits of faith in Christ, especially coupled with baptism in His Spirit. (See Acts 4:31.) To have access to the very throne room of God the Father Himself by Christ's blood is the foundation of all shelter from the storms; it stems from boldness in faith. It does not happen automatically; you must appropriate that shelter in boldness. Your faith in Jesus' blood redemption is the access point by which you push through the veil and "draw near with a true heart in full assurance of faith." Only then can you "hold fast" to the promises of God.

"Let us therefore come boldly to the throne of grace, that we may obtain mercy and find grace to help in time of need." (Hebrews 4:16) Shelter from the storm is yours for the taking—grab it by faith!

"Therefore, brethren, having boldness to enter the Holiest by the blood of Jesus, by a new and living way which He consecrated for us, through the veil, that is, His flesh, and having a High Priest over the house of God, let us draw near with a true heart in full assurance of faith, having our hearts sprinkled from an evil conscience and our bodies washed with pure water. Let us hold fast the confession of our hope without wavering, for He who promised is faithful."

Hebrews 10:19-23

You are saved by grace so that in Christ Jesus you may "... have boldness and access with confidence through faith in Him." (Ephesians 3:12) The purpose of the blood of Jesus is to "sprinkle" our hearts, minds (that's "conscience") and bodies, so that by faith in Him we are pure and can enter into God's throne room (the Holiest) with confidence that the King Himself will entertain our requests. The blood of Jesus covers every aspect of our existence: spirit, soul and body.

Once we have that boldness given by Christ's blood, we must "hold fast" our confession in hope. The faithful promises of God to carry us through and over the storms of life are contingent upon faith and boldness on our part. We cannot "waver" in our stance, so stand firm!

❧ Day 175 ❦

"My brethren, count it all joy when you fall into various trials, knowing that the testing of your faith produces patience. But let patience have its perfect work, that you may be perfect and complete, lacking nothing."

James 1:2-4

It seems counterintuitive to "count it all joy" during the trials of life. Worldly wisdom dictates that "misery loves company," so rather than rejoice, let's commiserate in our woes with everyone else. Of course there is benefit in finding comfort with a trusted friend or loved one during life-storms. Total isolation is unwise and not encouraged in the Bible. (See Hebrews 10:25.)

And yet, the Christian who is bold in faith, walking in love toward God and others, recognizes that it is only by pressure that patience is produced, and rather than finding an outlet for his or her own woes only, seeks to provide comfort for another even while undergoing trials of their own. James is asking the reader to consider (that's what "count" means in the Greek; Strong's #G2233) a shift in perspective: the testing of faith is a cause for rejoicing because it brings "perfection" of patience. We're not celebrating the trial itself; we are celebrating the result it produces, and that should bring us all comfort if we are operating with faith in the Lord's salvation.

❦ Day 176 ❦

"My brethren, count it all joy when you fall into various trials, knowing that the testing of your faith produces patience. But let patience have its perfect work, that you may be perfect and complete, lacking nothing."

James 1:2-4

Joy is a separate response to "various trials." God intends for you to be joyful in the midst of storms. That is not a contradiction—it is a supernatural, favorable response to natural, unfavorable circumstances. It does not mean you don't *also* feel the discomfort or ache in the trial, but you choose to focus on what is produced by the "testing of your faith": perfected, complete patience, which ensures you will lack nothing.

Without the trials, you cannot be perfected and complete. The trials themselves force us to draw near to God. (See Psalm 119:67,71.) So, since it's not a matter of *if* but *when* we fall into various trials, it is to our great advantage to have the appropriate response: keeping joyful. This produces Christlikeness in us, which is the entire point of this life: to "put on Christ" like we mentioned earlier. If you don't think that Jesus retained His joy during His trials, I refer you to Hebrews 12:1-2. The reward of faith, patience, endurance is certainly worth the trial to get it!

❧ Day 177 ❧

"For in it the righteousness of God is revealed from faith to faith; as it is written, 'The just shall live by faith.'"

Romans 1:17

*N*umerous interpretations exist concerning the somewhat confusing phrase "from faith to faith." To understand it better, we need to understand the "righteousness of God" revealed by the "it" mentioned right before, which, in turn, refers to the "gospel of Christ" in Verse 16. This righteousness isn't just God's own inherent righteousness as a product of His existence. He would still be righteous, even if no one else is. (See Romans 3:10.) But rather, this speaks to the righteousness imputed to the believer whose faith is put into the gospel of Jesus. They are granted Christ's righteousness by their belief in Him. (See 2 Corinthians 5:21; Romans 3:22.)

The literal phrase in the Greek is "from faith into faith." Some take this to mean progressing in faith, or levels of faith, and this is not wholly incorrect, but the intention appears to me to be "wholly by faith." Standing by faith from the beginning all the way to the end: from faith into faith. This means the shelter from the storm, which is a byproduct of the righteousness accredited to us by Christ, is only and always accessed by faith. So quite truly, "the just shall live by faith."

"For in it the righteousness of God is revealed from faith to faith; as it is written, 'The just shall live by faith.'"

Romans 1:17

Other interpretations of "from faith to faith" may also be correct. For example, the progression of faith, from "newborn" faith to fully mature faith as one grows in experiential knowledge, from the milk to the meat of the Word. (See 1 Corinthians 3:2.) This also implies testing, refining by fire, as mentioned in the discourse on James 1:2-4 earlier. Some would say it is faith in the Law (Old Testament) moving into faith in Christ (New Testament.) Or even the faith within a person responding to the faith within God. There's an element of truth in all these interpretations and could be applied to our concept of "shelter from the storm."

While I personally think the "entirely or completely by faith" rendering is perhaps the best, the application of this verse doesn't change significantly with any of the above interpretations. God's protection and provision to carry us through or over life-storms respond directly to *our faith* in Christ. They are not automatic just because one has a marginal relationship with the Lord. It takes our pressing into Him to make this shelter actualized. He provides the means by which we take that shelter by faith.

"Be strong and of good courage, do not fear nor be afraid of them; for the LORD your God, He is the One who goes with you. He will not leave you nor forsake you."

Deuteronomy 31:6

*H*e will not leave you nor forsake you" is a promise reiterated in Hebrews 13:5 and is just as applicable to us today as it was to the Israelites millennia ago. The "stick-to-it"-ness of God is an unfailing attribute as real as His righteousness, love, wrath and mercy. This verse promises that in any situation, no matter how dire it seems to you, God "goes with you" every step you take.

Jesus is the Friend who sticks closer than a brother mentioned in Proverbs 18:24. This is not vapid sentiment, some mawkish platitude given to placate people who are suffering; but rather, a promise from Almighty God that if you give Him everything you are, He promises to give you everything that He is.

If people truly understood this covenantal pledge and believed in its execution, they would be utterly fearless. No storm of life could shake them; they would not be moved no matter what rose up against them. Be strong and courageous, being convinced that this promise is made directly to you!

✼ *Day 180* ✾

"Be strong and of good courage, do not fear nor be afraid of them; for the Lord *your God, He is the One who goes with you. He will not leave you nor forsake you."*

Deuteronomy 31:6

*L*eave you" in the Hebrew is a word that signifies "dropped from the hand." (Strong's #H7503) Literally, to "slacken or sink down" or "to be idle." It's rendered "fail you" in the KJV. *Forsake* means "abandoned, neglected, deserted, left behind." (Strong's #H5800) "Do not fear nor be afraid" sounds like repetition, but one word in the Hebrew means *fear* as we know it to mean, also with the added understanding of "revere or be in awe of, astonished." (Strong's #H3372) The other word means "to be broken by terror, to tremble with dread." (Strong's #H6206)

We have to give in to none of this fear because the Lord God is the One who goes with us. That is the word for "walk" (Strong's #H1980) and is the same one used in Genesis 3:8 and whenever the Bible says someone "walked with God." To be weak and cowardly—the opposite of strong and of good courage—in the face of difficulties when we have a Companion like that walking with us is not only insulting to Him but nonsensical for us. Keep this promise in the forefront of your thinking with every storm you encounter!

❧ Day 181 ❦

"The Lord is my shepherd; I shall not want. He makes me to lie down in green pastures; He leads me beside the still waters. He restores my soul; He leads me in the paths of righteousness for His name's sake. Yea, though I walk through the valley of the shadow of death, I will fear no evil; for You are with me; Your rod and Your staff, they comfort me. You prepare a table before me in the presence of my enemies; You anoint my head with oil; my cup runs over. Surely goodness and mercy shall follow me all the days of my life; and I will dwell in the house of the Lord forever."

Psalm 23

Psalm 23 is perhaps the most famous chapter in the Bible. It's so much more than just a "pretty piece of poetry." The power inherent in the inspired words provide more than some vague level of comfort in the midst of distress—they outline everything the Lord has for His people: a lack of want, clear direction, peace, courage, righteousness, safety, comfort, material provision, anointing, surplus, goodness and mercy, a place to dwell with Him forever. Nothing you are going through is left to chance; God will supply every need! (Philippians 4:19) This psalm is the declaration of all the shelter from the storms God provides to you, summing up everything shared in the course of this book!

❦ Day 182 ❦

*"The L*ORD *is my shepherd; I shall not want. He makes me to lie down in green pastures; He leads me beside the still waters. He restores my soul; He leads me in the paths of righteousness for His name's sake. Yea, though I walk through the valley of the shadow of death, I will fear no evil; for You are with me; Your rod and Your staff, they comfort me. You prepare a table before me in the presence of my enemies; You anoint my head with oil; my cup runs over. Surely goodness and mercy shall follow me all the days of my life; and I will dwell in the house of the L*ORD *forever."*

Psalm 23

*Y*ehovah Ra'ah (Strong's #H3068; #H7462) is a covenantal name of God revealed in this psalm. It speaks of being a "special Friend," a "boon Companion." His friendship grants to us *rest* and *relaxation*. In the midst of stormy weather, you can have green pastures and still waters. As He leads you into righteousness (that is, going the "right way"), He *restores* or *refreshes* your soul. He *removes* fear because of His love for you. (1 John 4:18) He *reassures* you in comfort. He *reinvigorates* you by providing material needs and sustenance. Surely goodness and mercy will follow you day-by-day! In summation, He *is* your Shelter from the storm, the Answer to every problem you could ever face! Amen.

About the Authors

ANDREW & CHRISTY MALONEY are the authors of *Eight Weeks with No Water*, a testimony of their second son's miraculous birth. Stemming from their upbringing in families that put the highest emphasis on a relationship with the Lord, they have a passion to share the Word of God to a hurting world and see His power change lives. They live in the crosstimbers area of North Texas with their two sons, Connor and Christian.

To reach the authors, please visit www.doveontherise.com.

Printed in the United States
By Bookmasters